PETERSON'S

PERFECT

PERSONAL

STATEMENTS

LAW ■ BUSINESS
MEDICAL ■ GRADUATE SCHOOL

Third Edition

Mark Alan Stewart

PETERSON'S

A **nelnet.** COMPANY

PETERSON'S

A (n)el net. COMPANY

About Peterson's, a Nelnet company

Peterson's (www.petersons.com) is a leading provider of education information and advice, with books and online resources focusing on education search, test preparation, and financial aid. Its Web site offers searchable databases and interactive tools for contacting educational institutions, online practice tests and instruction, and planning tools for securing financial aid. Peterson's serves 110 million education consumers annually.

For more information, contact Peterson's, 2000 Lenox Drive, Lawrenceville, NJ 08648; 800-338-3282; or find us on the World Wide Web at www.petersons.com.

ISBN 13: 978-0-7689-1715-4
ISBN 10: 0-7689-1715-8

Printed in Canada

10 9 8 7 6 5 4   09 08 07

Third Edition

Acknowledgments

The author gratefully acknowledges the following successful graduate- and professional-schoool applicants who contributed their personal statements to this publication:

Arman Afagh, pp. 56, 81
Roger Barone, p. 54
Craig Black, p. 69
Andrew Boer, p. 59
Eric Brock, pp. 77, 78
David T. Burrell, p. 64
Arun Chandra, p. 62
Dave Hitch, p. 48
Eric Henry, p. 65
Brady Ho, pp. 66, 88
Ian Kasper, p. 79
Paul Lacourciere, p. 50
Susan Lasley, p. 75
Ruth Lufkin, pp. 57, 70
Piroz Mohseni, p. 67
Adam Muchnick, p. 83
Nathaniel Olsson, pp. 79, 86
Tara Prigge, p. 60
Dave Ray, p. 46
David Schoenthal, p. 72
Mark Siegel, p. 82
Kenneth Simon, p. 87
Julie Wiskirchen, pp. 45, 74

About the Author

Mark Alan Stewart (B.A., Economics, J.D., University of California at Los Angeles) is an attorney and one of today's preeminent authorities and top-selling authors on the subject of graduate-level admissions. For more than a decade Mr. Stewart served as consultant to schools in the University of California and California State University systems in graduate-level entrance-exam programs. His books on GMAT, LSAT, and GRE preparation continue to be top sellers among aspiring business, law, and graduate students. His other book-length publications for graduate-level admissions (all published by Peterson's) include the following:

Writing Skills for the GRE/GMAT
The Ultimate GMAT Tool Kit
GMAT CAT—Answers to the Real Essay Questions
GRE—Answers to the Real Essay Questions
30 Days to the LSAT
30 Days to the GMAT CAT
GRE-LSAT Logic Workbook
GRE-LSAT-GMAT-MCAT Reading Comprehension Workbook
Words for Smart Test-Takers
Math for Smart Test-Takers

Online Updates for *Perfect Personal Statements*
The author's Internet Edition of *Perfect Personal Statements* (www.west. net/~stewart/pps) provides updates and supplements to this book, as well as links to supplements for some of the other books listed above.

Contents

PART 3

THIRTY GREAT PERSONAL STATEMENTS (BY SUCCESSFUL APPLICANTS) 44

PART 4

ADVICE FROM THE EXPERTS 92

Undergraduate Grades and Entrance-Exam Scores Don't Tell the Whole Story

The admission process for graduate and professional school is more competitive today than ever before. The increase in applications to these schools has been especially dramatic in recent years, due to a shrinking entry-level job market for recent college graduates. The number of applications to U.S. medical schools for the 1994–95 year was nearly twice that for 1989–90! Schools are flooded with applications from many well-qualified candidates whose entrance-exam scores and undergraduate grades are almost identical. Admissions officials recognize that the "numbers"—GPA and entrance-exam scores—don't tell the whole story about any candidate. The schools are looking for more than proficient test-takers. They are also looking for people who are interesting, articulate, and distinctive, with different points of view, ambitions, backgrounds, and interests. A diverse and interesting student body enriches the academic experience for everyone—students, faculty, and administration. And it is interesting and distinctive people, not necessarily those who perform well on exams, who are likely to succeed in the long run in their chosen professions. (The admissions and alumni offices are symbiotically connected, and they know it.)

How do the decision-makers look at the human being behind the application? The answer: through essay questions on the admissions application, commonly referred to as *personal statements*, as well as through *letters of recommendation* and *in-person interviews*. Don't panic. There's plenty of help at hand—right here. This book will demystify these critical aspects of the admissions process. Here you will learn:

- How to create and write personal statements that respond to the questions that appear on the applications of many popular graduate schools

- Whom to approach for letters of recommendation

- How to make the best impression at your interview

In addition, you'll see 30 actual personal statements from successful graduate- and professional-school applicants. And you'll get inside advice about the entire admissions process from admissions officials at top schools from coast to coast!

PART 1

Creating Perfect Personal Statements

The "personal statement" portion of a school's admissions application presents a great opportunity for you to sell yourself to the school. However, this critical part of the application can be a source of great anxiety and worry for the applicant, who may wonder:

- Who will read my essay?
- How will my essay be evaluated?
- Should I just play it safe and say what they want to hear? If so, what exactly do they want to hear?
- Should I take a risk and submit something that is sure to make the admissions committee notice me? If so, how can I ensure that I don't offend committee members or turn them off?
- Should I discuss that glaring blemish in my past, or should I ignore it?

Turning such questions over in your mind can paralyze you. Moreover, because the questions posed in the applications are generally very open-ended, after writing your personal statement you may still wonder whether your statement is appropriate and effective—that is, whether it will help you to gain admission. To solve these problems, you simply need more information about the admissions process. Let's begin by looking at personal-statement questions that are typically posed on admissions applications.

THE QUESTIONS

The particular essay questions appearing on the applications vary widely among the schools. Some applications provide very little guidance as to what you should write. Others include specific questions. While some schools impose a word or page limit on your response, others do not. Some schools require only one personal statement, while others might require several essay responses. Some schools require a mandatory statement as well as one or more optional essays. The following list is a representative sampling of the sorts of questions appearing on graduate- and professional-school applications.

✎ TOPICS THAT ARE EXTREMELY OPEN-ENDED

"Provide any additional information you wish to bring to the attention of the Admission Committee. You may wish to discuss particular accomplishments, activities, employment, hobbies, or professional goals."

"We require all applicants to submit a personal statement. The statement should describe any unusual aspects of your background which might contribute to the diversity of our student body as well as describe any extraordinary skills or traits that you might possess which would be relevant to us."

"Please submit a personal statement not exceeding 500 words in length on a matter that interests you."

✎ TOPICS THAT CALL FOR YOU TO DISCUSS YOUR PAST EXPERIENCES

"Please discuss any significant activities or work experience which might enrich your study at our school."

"Describe an experience (either personal or professional) in which you failed. What did you learn from that experience?"

✎ TOPICS THAT INQUIRE ABOUT YOUR MOTIVES, GOALS, AND AMBITIONS

"Tell us your reasons for seeking a professional education."

"At this point in your life, what motivates you to consider further education at our school?"

"Discuss the aspects of your background and experience that have led you to choose a career in . . ."

"This statement is your opportunity to introduce yourself to the admissions committee and to discuss your personal and professional goals."

"How would you want your professional achievements and contributions to be remembered after your death?"

"Discuss how a degree from our school/program will assist you in reaching your short- and long-term goals."

✎ TOPICS THAT REQUIRE SELF-ASSESSMENT OR INSIGHT ABOUT YOUR PERSONALITY

"Please comment on your strengths and weaknesses in certain courses or activities."

"Discuss an ethical dilemma you have faced and how you dealt with it."

"If you could have dinner with any three people (alive now or from another era), who would they be and what would you hope to learn from them?"

✎ TOPICS THAT INVITE YOU TO EXPLAIN BLEMISHES, DEFICIENCIES, OR GAPS IN YOUR PAST

"If you are unable to submit the minimum number of recommendation forms that we request, please give your reasons."

"Please explain anything in your application that does not accurately reflect your abilities or potential for successful graduate study."

"Discuss any unique aspect of your personal or professional background that may not be adequately presented elsewhere in this application."

The questions also vary somewhat according to the type of program (law, business, medicine, or graduate study).

Law Schools

Because law is a highly verbal pursuit—academically and professionally—law schools even more than other schools read personal statements for evidence of the applicant's ability to communicate effectively in writing and to reason well. So for law schools, what is distinctive is not so much their questions as what they look for in a response.

Business Schools

Applications to graduate business schools tend to include questions designed to assess the applicant's potential as a manager, leader, and team member. Here are some common examples:

> "Describe a situation in which you were compelled to take a stand against the majority. How did this experience strengthen your understanding of leadership?"

> "Discuss a significant accomplishment that demonstrates your potential as a leader and a manager."

> "Describe a situation in which you were part of a group working to solve a problem and your contribution to that goal."

Medical Schools

The standard AMCAS application requires a very open-ended "Personal Comments" essay. Supplemental applications from the schools tend to ask very pointed questions about past activities.

Non-Professional Graduate Programs

Applications typically require a "Statement of Purpose" in which the applicant is asked to discuss his or her areas of academic/research interest as well as long-term plans.

PREPARING TO WRITE YOUR ESSAYS

Writing an effective personal statement requires a bit of soul-searching and reflection. The schools want to gain from your essay some insight into your character and personality. It's difficult for most people to write about themselves, especially something personal or introspective. The following suggestions may help your creative juices to flow so that you can get started.

1. **Consult Friends and Relatives for Ideas**
   Others see us differently from the way we see ourselves. You may be overlooking some theme, angle, or aspect of your personality that might be obvious to others who know you well. Good ideas are good ideas, whatever their source.

2. **Take Inventory of Your Unique Experiences, Major Influences, and Abilities**

   Don't discount anything. You may think that your artistic ability, that summer trip to Europe, or that great book you read recently is irrelevant or unimportant, but it's not. Carry a note pad around with you for a few months and jot down anything that comes to mind. Don't evaluate its usefulness before writing it down. Just write it down.

3. **Write an Experimental Creative Essay in Which You Are the Main Character**

   Pretend that you are enrolled in a creative writing class and that your assignment is to write a moving and inspiring short story (a couple of pages) about some experience in your life and its impact on you. Pretend you will be reading the story aloud during class and that your goal is to have your classmates approach you afterward with the following sorts of reactions: "I feel as if I know you, even though I've never talked to you before" or "I was really moved; thanks for taking a risk and giving us a glimpse into what makes you tick." Lest you think this is a silly exercise, read the interviews with admissions officials later in this book, and you will discover how close your successful short story is to what the schools are looking for in a good personal statement.

4. **Assemble Your Applications and Determine How Many Different Essays You Must Write**

   The schools are concerned that you address their specific essay topic(s) and their particular school (except that the AMCAS personal comments for medical-school admission are written for all participating schools). This is not to say, however, that you will be required to write entirely different essays for each and every school to which you apply. The schools ask similar questions, and you will probably be able to submit essentially the same essay to multiple schools. By taking inventory of all of the different essay questions for all of your applications, you will see that the task is not as daunting is it might first have appeared.

5. **Get Feedback From Others Before Completing Your Final Draft**

   It's easy to lose objectivity or to overlook errors, inconsistencies, or problems when you have focused too intensely or for too long on a particular task. You may have revised your essay so many times that you have forgotten what the question is, and your essay no longer adequately responds to it. Or you may have crafted what you think is a witty and clever remark or an eloquent statement, while in reality you have just written something rather corny or inappropriate. Also, even the best writers make grammatical and typographical errors, and spell-checking and grammar-checking software won't reveal every problem. Before typing that final version, by all means show your essays to a few other people—perhaps your peers or faculty adviser—for their feedback.

WRITING YOUR PERSONAL STATEMENT—CONTENT AND THEME

Whether your personal statement makes a positive or negative impression, or no impression at all, depends on your judgment in deciding (1) what to write about, (2) how to write about it, and (3) how you present what you have to say to the reader. A good judgment call may result in a distinctive essay that wins over the reader, while an error in judgment may result in a distinctively *inappropriate* essay that makes a negative impression. Consider the following advice regarding content and theme as well the guidelines later in Part 1 regarding style, format, and presentation.

✎ THE ULTIMATE TEST FOR CONTENT

Your personal statement must, of course, be tailored to the requirements of the particular application. However, as you know from our earlier discussion, the question may invite you to discuss virtually *anything* about yourself that you want the reader to know. So what *should* you talk about, and what should you *not* talk about? One fundamental point of advice applies in every situation. Put your essay to the ultimate test, by asking yourself:

Is this essay one that *only I* could honestly write?

Is it possible that other applicants could have honestly said essentially the same things that you have said in your essay? Take a yellow highlighter or other pen and mark every sentence of your essay that another applicant might honestly have written. Do you see a lot of yellow? If so, you either need to dig deeper (stay with the same theme but bring it down to a more personal level) or go back to the drawing board and find a different theme or topic—one that you know only *you* will be writing about.

WHAT THEY ARE *REALLY* LOOKING FOR

Any admissions official will tell you that there really is no right or wrong response. Okay, that's probably good to know but not all that helpful. Let's dig a bit deeper. After reading the interviews in Part 4, you will agree that, more than anything else, the schools are looking for some insight into your *persona*; they are hoping to get a glimpse of the human being behind the data in your file. Your essay should evoke a mental image of your personality. Remember that the personal statement is an interview of sorts. What is it about your personality that strikes people as particularly attractive or interesting? Is it your sense of humor? Your boldness? Your sensitivity? Your humility? Your imagination? Your spirit? Your way with words? Ask your friends for their impressions, and try to convey your persona through your personal statement, either by the way you write or by what you write about.

ALMOST EVERYONE MAKES THIS MISTAKE

On the basis of the interviews conducted for this book, I can confidently say that the most common personal-statement blunder is to write an expository resume of your background and experience. This is not to say that the schools are not interested in your accomplishments. However, other portions of your application will provide this information, and the reader does not want to read your life story in narrative form. Strive for depth, not breadth. An effective personal statement will focus on one or two specific themes, incidents, or points. Don't try to cram too much into your essay.

GETTING CREATIVE—ESPECIALLY IN YOUR OPENING REMARKS

In the interest of submitting a distinctive essay, how creative should you get in terms of content? Particularly for more open-ended questions, the personal statement is your opportunity to captivate the reader, if only for a few minutes. Exercise your creativity and tell a compelling short story in which you are the main character. This does not mean that you should write a work of fiction. However, an unusual story that is colorfully and imaginatively crafted makes for a memorable and impressive personal statement.

The opening sentences of your essay are particularly critical in capturing the reader's curiosity, attention, and interest. Your opener should tease the reader, enticing him or her to read on. Consider opening with an amusing personal anecdote, an observation from "out in left field," or a bold and perhaps *mildly* provocative statement. You might try beginning your essay by posing an interesting question that compels the reader to continue reading in order to find out the answer. Several of the sample essays in Part 3 use attention-grabbing openers to capture the reader's interest.

✎ TAKING RISKS IN EXPRESSING YOURSELF

Should you take a risk and submit something a bit off-the-wall or controversial, or should you play it safe and write a conservative essay that will offend no one but may look a lot like those of everyone else? Don't be reluctant to express your opinions, as long as they are well-reasoned. The readers respect and admire independent thought and boldness. Be careful, however, not to make inflammatory statements just to grab the reader's attention; you may risk appearing fanatical or intolerant.

Finally, whether you "play it safe" may depend on how you assess your chances of gaining admission based upon other aspects of your application. If you are a "shoo-in," why not submit a conservative essay and focus your efforts on applications to those schools at which your chances are slimmer?

✎ DISCUSSING YOUR BACKGROUND AND EXPERIENCE

If the question calls for you to discuss your background and experience, there is nothing wrong with recounting key academic accomplishments, extracurricular activities, work experience, or community involvement. However, you must try to distinguish your essay from all the others by digging a bit deeper—discuss how a specific experience contributed to your values, outlook, ambitions, and concerns. In other words, rather than just recounting an experience, *evaluate* it in terms of who you are as a person right now. Also remember that the reader may be reading hundreds of other essays as well. Your challenge, then, is to capture his or her interest. Tell a brief story with a clear, coherent, and distinctive theme. Here are some examples.

- Relate a particular experience and explain how it contributed to your sense of social commitment

- Talk about what you learned about yourself (e.g., your strengths or limitations) from the particular experience that has made you a better person—more mature, more self-confident, better suited for your chosen career path, etc.

- Demonstrate your tenacity by discussing one or two situations in which you succeeded in the face of adversity

Consider discussing the more personal areas of your life that might give the reader a better look at what drives you—what makes you "tick." Use your essay as a vehicle for conveying the qualities you have that the school may be looking for. To help you think of ideas, review the list of character traits on page 32–33. This list tells you more specifically the sorts of qualities that the schools are looking for in their students.

✎ DISCUSSING WHAT MAKES YOU DIFFERENT OR UNIQUE

A school might ask how you can add to the *diversity* of the student body. Many applicants look very much alike, however, in terms of academic, work, and other life experiences. So how should you respond if you don't think there is anything especially unique, distinctive, or unusual about you? First, if your response to such a question is optional, you might consider opting out. Otherwise, you might be surprised at what you can dig up about yourself to discuss if you put your mind to it. Here's a short list that might help you begin your brainstorming session and set your wheels in motion:

- Your family (spouse, parents, children, even pets)

- Your role models and inspirations

- The time you helped a friend through a personal trauma (or vice versa)

- The remote place where you spent a portion of your formative years

- The trophies on your mantle

- That picture on the wall of you shaking the hand of someone famous

- That newspaper clipping about you that you keep in your scrapbook

- Your unusual (perhaps quirky) skills, talents, and abilities

- A learning disability

- A physical handicap or other feature that might make you different

- Your disadvantaged background or minority status

The last three items listed above deserve special attention and need to be discussed in more detail here.

✎ DISCUSSING YOUR MINORITY STATUS OR DISADVANTAGED BACKGROUND

Perhaps you have been disadvantaged socioeconomically at some point in your life. Consider using your personal statement to discuss how you (and/or your family) overcame or are trying to overcome that disadvantage. Some of the most compelling essays that the schools see are on this theme. Be careful, however, not to blame others for your problems. The personal statement is not the place for whining and complaining about your circumstances in life.

There is no hard-and-fast rule about whether you should discuss your minority status. If you can tell a compelling story about it or if it relates directly to your motives and career goals, then by all means write about it. Otherwise, you might be better off focusing on some other theme.

✎ DISCUSSING YOUR MOTIVES AND ASPIRATIONS

The schools obviously seek individuals who are serious about graduate study, who are properly motivated, and who will represent the school well by their professional contributions. Accordingly, a school may invite you to use your personal statement as an opportunity to talk about your motives, plans, goals, and ambitions. Some of the more common concerns about this type of essay are addressed below.

Commitment to a Social Cause, Ideology, or Religion

Perhaps you are pursuing further education in order to make the world a better place to live. What would the admissions committee think of your idealism? If you are going to get up on a soapbox and tell the reader how you hope to contribute to world peace or prevent environmental devastation or human injustice, you had better have a *demonstrated* commitment to your cause. Anyone can say anything about motives, but what have you *done* lately? If you can point out particular academic pursuits, work experience (paid or volunteer), community activities, or other experience that corroborates your claim, then discuss it. Otherwise, find another angle.

While we are on the subject of dreaming, do not talk about your dream of becoming the President of the United States or the next Bill Gates or Jonas Salk. Even if you believe your lofty goal to be within the realm of possibility, you will be giving the reader reason to question your common sense.

If your religious faith is an integral motive for pursuing further education and for your long-term career goals, should you discuss this? If you are applying for admission to a program in philosophy or religious studies or if the school to which you are applying is a private religious school, of course it would be entirely appropriate to discuss how your personal religious beliefs and faith enter into your decision. Otherwise, it is probably best to avoid a sensitive issue like religion, even if your faith is at the core of your desire to enter a particular profession or field of study. The reader may be someone who is very turned off by a spiritual "angle." If you must discuss your religious background or beliefs, tread gingerly and be careful not to offend. (Part 3 includes essays from applicants who successfully did so.)

Discussing the Financial Rewards of Your Chosen Career

If your desire to command a high salary in the working world is part of your motivation, don't admit it. Admissions officials—especially at professional schools—are well aware that socioeconomic status is a big motivating factor for many applicants. By taking this angle in your personal statement, you would be telling the reader essentially that you are very much like most other applicants. In a competitive process in which you hope to distinguish yourself from the crowd, this angle wouldn't help much, would it?

Leaving an Unsatisfying Career in Pursuit of Another One

Perhaps you are a second-career applicant making a life change, and your desire to discontinue your present work is your prime motivation for pursuing further education. Would it be appropriate to take this approach in your personal statement? Probably not. The fact that you are a returning student may help set you apart from other applicants in some positive ways. However, being miserable in your current circumstance is not really positive, is it?

Focus on the affirmative in your personal statement. Okay, so you want to make a career change. Why this direction rather than some other? There must be something in your experience or your thinking that has prompted you to turn in a particular direction. Figure out what it is and talk about that. If the career path that you are now seeking is entirely inconsistent with your educational and employment history, do not point this out to the reader. Instead, focus on how this new career path is consistent with your hopes, your true talents, your genuine interests, certain past activities, and so forth.

Lack of Clarity about Career Goals

Perhaps you have no concrete ideas about what you want to do after graduate school. How should you respond to a question that asks about your career goals? There's nothing wrong with admitting that your goals are a bit unclear. Many aspiring graduate- and professional-school students, especially those recently in college, are quite unsure of their motives and ambitions. The reader will probably appreciate your candor. In fact, if you outline a very specific plan for your future, the reader may suspect that you are either making it up for his or her benefit or that you are too narrow in your focus. Either impression might adversely affect your chance of admission. Offer the reader two or three general scenarios for your future to demonstrate that you are broad-minded and flexible about your career path. In Part 3 of this book, you will see several sample essays that illustrate this advice.

✎ DISCUSSING WHY YOU WANT TO ATTEND THIS PARTICULAR SCHOOL

Address each particular school individually rather than writing a "canned" essay and submitting it to multiple schools. Discuss your reasons for choosing the particular school over others, whether or not the school explicitly asks for your reasons (most do not). Whether your explanation will help or hurt your chances of admission may very well depend upon what those reasons are.

Discussing the School's Rank or Prestige

Many applicants select the schools to which they apply based largely on their ranking by various well-known independent reports. If you are among these applicants, should you admit it? Definitely not, if doing so would be to state explicitly that you are interested in a particular school because of its prominent position in the rankings. The schools are aware of reports such as the *Gourman Report*, and they are all too aware that applicants quite often select schools based upon these reports. Talk about the school itself, not about what someone else has reported about the school.

Discussing the Not-So-Unique Features of a Particular School

Many schools ask in their applications why you are selecting their particular school over other similar programs. Perhaps all you know about the school is what the catalog states and what you've heard from a few people who attended the school. How should you respond? First, avoid merely restating what is already in the school's catalog or repeating secondhand information. Also avoid vague generalizations about the school. Consider, for example, the following statements that admissions officials see in one form or another all the time:

"I want to attend your school because . . .

. . . it is a nationally recognized school with a top-notch reputation"

. . . you have a strong faculty"

. . . you have a strong endowment and extensive research facilities"

. . . you have a strong clinical or cooperative program"

. . . your school has a well-connected alumni network"

Anyone can make these claims about a lot of schools, and you are wasting your personal-statement opportunity unless you also discuss specifically how the school is strong in a certain area and why this feature is particularly important to you in terms of your goals and interests. And don't stop short in your explanation. The following statements are too vague and will not provide useful information to the reader:

"I am particularly interested in your clinical and cooperative program because I think it is important to participate in hands-on activities that complement the more theoretical classroom discussion."

"Your strong alumni network is important because it would broaden my career opportunities."

"The strength of your faculty will help me get the most out of my academic experience."

Again, anyone can make these kinds of claims. Dig deeper; get specific.

Discussing the Campus Environment, Climate, Etc.

Perhaps you are applying to one particular school because you like the campus, the environment, and the climate. Would it be legitimate for you to discuss these reasons in your personal statement? There are cases where it would be quite appropriate to talk about the school's location as a factor in your school selection. If you are applying for graduate study in geology or oceanography, for example, the natural environment would be important to you. For programs in architecture and art history or musicology, the region's cultural endowments would legitimately enter into your decision. For international business, a cosmopolitan urban setting would be ideal. Perhaps you are applying to a fine arts program in which creativity and inspiration depend upon your visual surroundings.

Otherwise, be careful about discussing environment as a motivating factor for you. Good weather is nice but may distract you from your studies, so don't admit that climate is a factor in your decision. As for the campus itself, there are a lot of attractive campuses. So what? It's probably best to keep your impressions of the campus to yourself. As for the romantic allure of a "big-city" or "small-town" environment, why not just move there and get a job instead of pursuing graduate study?

Discussing Faculty, Student Organizations, Etc.

Get specific about the school by talking about how you would like to study under particular faculty members or why you would like to be involved in a particular student organization or activity. This will help you to stand out among other applicants. Perhaps you can identify particular faculty whose areas of research coincide with your areas of interest. Consider contacting one or two faculty members first and discuss with them their current research projects and your interest in studying under them. Then refer to your contacts in your essay. The professors will probably be flattered, and the reader will be impressed at your thoroughness, assertiveness, and industry. However, be careful that your discussion doesn't appear contrived or insincere. The reader should be able to corroborate your supposed areas of interest with your previous activities as set forth in your application. As for discussing your interest in particular student organizations or activities, is the organization or activity unique to this school? If so, then talk about. However, if most schools have a similar organization, consider bypassing the topic.

✎ EXPLAINING DEFICIENCIES, INCONSISTENCIES, AND BLEMISHES

Certain aspects of your application may call for an explanation. Such aspects might include any of the following:

- Undergraduate grades

- Entrance exam scores

- Deficiency in the number of letters of recommendation submitted

- Lack of work experience

- Lack of extracurricular activities

- Why you are applying again after being denied previously

- Gaps in the chronological account of your education or employment

- Disciplinary action by an institution of higher education

- Criminal record

Under what circumstances should you use your personal statement to explain a particular deficiency, weakness, or other blemish? First of all, the application might explicitly invite you to explain deficiencies, weaknesses, aberrations, or any other aspect of the application that might not accurately reflect your abilities or potential and fitness for graduate study. Schools almost without exception ask specifically about the last two items above (see *Disclosing Skeletons in Your Closet*, below). For the other items, where applications do not explicitly provide for such explanations, the schools nevertheless permit and generally encourage applicants to provide brief explanations. Most schools suggest that you attach an *addendum* to your personal statement for this purpose while reserving the personal statement itself for positive information about yourself. If you are in doubt about the policy and preferred procedure of a particular school, contact the school directly.

If you feel compelled to explain that subpar GPA during your freshman year or that one course you withdrew from with a failing grade, try to transform such blemishes into something positive by pointing out particular courses in which you performed well, especially those that were more advanced, more relevant to your intended career path, or more recent.

✎ DISCLOSING SKELETONS IN YOUR CLOSET

Perhaps you were once the subject of disciplinary action at your undergraduate college. Should you inform the school about this in your application? If so, should you include this discussion in your personal statement? In all likelihood, the application will inquire about academic discipline as well as criminal record. You will undoubtedly be denied admission (or expelled if you are already matriculating) if the school discovers that you have intentionally concealed disciplinary action or criminal conviction. The admissions committee may very well overlook that indiscretion of youth (e.g., during your freshman year of college) if you bring it into the open and explain the circumstances. Many applicants do not fully appreciate that admissions officials make every effort to afford applicants the benefit of the doubt in such cases.

✎ DISCUSSING YOUR RECOMMENDERS AND OTHER "INFLUENTIAL" PEOPLE

Most schools require one or more letters of recommendation, and you should choose your recommenders carefully (see Part 2). Think about who your recommenders are, and ask yourself whether the admissions committee might wonder why you chose who you did. Your choice of recommenders may be quite logical and require no explanation. On the other hand, if you think your choice might call for an explanation, by all means give one, preferably in an addendum to your personal statement. Also, if you are submitting fewer than the minimum number of letters required by the school, by all means explain this in an addendum. Admissions officials may overlook such a deficiency if you have a good reason for it. In any event, don't ignore it.

What about mentioning "influential" people—for example, alumni friends and relatives or public figures—to impress or sway the admissions committee? Unless the school asks specifically about alumni connections (some private schools ask the applicant to list family members who are alumni), avoid name dropping. Any impression you make by attempting to persuade the admissions committee in this manner will in all likelihood be a negative one.

WRITING YOUR PERSONAL STATEMENT—STYLE AND FORMAT

You should be concerned not only with the content of your personal statement but also with ensuring that it is presented appropriately. Of course you should proofread carefully to be certain that there are no typographical errors. Also, since you may be using the same *basic* personal statement in applying to multiple schools, be careful not to address the school by the wrong name. Beyond these obvious words of advice, there are numerous judgment calls that you must make in trying to capture the attention of the reader in a positive way.

✎ INTRODUCTORY PARAGRAPHS AND CONCLUSIONS/ SUMMARIES

Most of us have learned that a good essay includes an introduction and a conclusion—bookends that tie the package neatly together and allow the reader to anticipate and to recall. However, essays for graduate admission are generally not long enough to warrant a full-blown introduction or conclusion. In fact, you are really wasting your personal-statement opportunity as well as the reader's time by including an introduction or a conclusion just for the sake of doing so. Certainly you should avoid such conventional *introductions* as these:

"Allow me to introduce myself. My name is . . ."

"This question asks me to discuss . . ."

Also avoid hackneyed *concluding* remarks such as:

"I would like to thank the admissions committee for considering my application."

"It is my sincere hope that you will grant me the opportunity to attend your fine school."

"In sum, there are three reasons why you should admit me . . ."

Many applicants begin or end their personal statement by quoting a philosopher, literary figure, or other well-known observer of human affairs. The quotation is typically used to sum up the applicant's own personal philosophy or outlook. Beginning an essay in this way can be an effective way to capture the reader's attention. If you wish to use this angle, keep in mind that a lot of other applicants will be using the same angle. My personal view is that quotations are crutches; you should not rely on the words of others to express your thoughts for you. If you must resort to this angle, however, be sure to choose a relatively obscure quotation. Imagine using the same quotation as several other applicants. It happens!

✎ UNCONVENTIONAL AND GIMMICKY WRITING STYLES

Your "clever" or "original" idea for style probably isn't, and it may not be appreciated. Some of the more common "original" ideas that the schools see all the time are discussed below.

Referring to Yourself in the Third Person

Some applicants feel compelled for whatever reason to write about themselves as if they were writing about somebody else—for example, "Robert would like to attend your university because. . . ." Admissions officials strongly prefer the use of the first person (for example, "I would like to attend your university because . . .").

Trying to Impress the Reader with Your Linguistic Prowess

Choose words that real people actually use in formal writing. Attempts to impress with your knowledge of the English language are obvious and detract from the content of your essay. The reader will not thank you for improving his or her vocabulary. Moreover, if you can't use common words to express yourself adequately, this doesn't say much for your mastery of the English language, does it?

Trying to Impress the Reader with Your Knowledge of Technical Terminology

The personal statement is not the place to demonstrate your knowledge of an academic discipline or your proficiency with the peculiar jargon of the field. For example, if you are applying to law school, avoid using any words or phrases that smack of legalese.

Submitting an Essay in Rhyme or Other Form Besides Prose

Even if you are applying for admission to a program in creative writing, the personal statement is not the place for this kind of creativity. The schools are interested in your substantive response to their specific questions. A highly unconventional style may give them reason to question your judgment.

✎ UNCONVENTIONAL AND GIMMICKY FORMATS AND PACKAGES

In an attempt to be noticed, some applicants will resort to any means to draw the attention of the admissions officials. The schools have seen everything: essays on audiotape and videotape, on parchment scrolls, in bound leather volumes, and in calligraphy. Some law-school applicants submit essays that have the appearance of a court document. Some medical-school applicants submit essays that have the appearance of a diagnosis (complete with "indications" and "contraindications"). Some business-school applicants submit essays in the form of a corporate prospectus. As in the case of unconventional styles, there is no such thing as an "original" format or package, and your attempt to grab the reader's attention will probably not be appreciated; moreover, the use of a highly inappropriate gimmick may call into question your judgment, thereby weighing negatively on your application. The schools are not prepared to handle statements on audiotape or videotape and will most likely ask you to resubmit your essays in a conventional format.

✎ TYPEFACE, TYPE SIZE, AND HANDWRITTEN ESSAYS (PAPER-BASED APPLICATIONS ONLY)

Regarding your choice of typeface and point size, the key is readability. Remember that the reader might be reading literally hundreds of application essays and will appreciate high readability. Some typefaces are more readable in large blocks of text than others. Your typeface should not be too narrow, since narrow typefaces are difficult to read. Use a point size of 11 to 12, depending on the particular typeface (some typefaces look larger than others).

Do not submit a handwritten essay unless the school specifically requests it (a few medical schools do) or you are applying for admission to a graduate program in calligraphy (I bet you aren't). The schools do not appreciate this personal touch, even if your handwriting is beautiful.

✎ PAGE LIMITS AND WORD LIMITS

Imposing a word limit or a page limit on paper-based applications allows a school to process more applications in a shorter time. Thus, "high volume" schools are more likely to impose such limits. By imposing page and word limits, the school can also gauge your ability to follow directions and operate within the rules. You will not be automatically disqualified merely for exceeding a word or page limit on a personal statement, but complete disregard for directions may well affect your chances of admission.

While nobody will actually count your *words*, it will be rather obvious if you exceed a page limit. Some schools that impose a page limit simply do not read beyond the specified number of pages; others will read further but only to a point. Thus, if you have something brilliant to say on the third page of your personal statement, but the limit is two pages, your third page might go unread.

If a school imposes a page limit but does not provide any guidelines for margin size, point size, and spacing between lines, it may be tempting to reduce these specifications to fit more onto a page. Remember, however, that the key is *readability*. Use normal single spacing (default settings in word-processing programs) unless the school specifies otherwise, with margins of at least one-half inch on all sides. Also, do not try to save space by combining paragraphs; appropriate paragraphs enhance readability and comprehension.

✎ OBTAINING ASSISTANCE IN WRITING/EDITING YOUR PERSONAL STATEMENT

Perhaps your writing skills are somewhat weak and you don't want to make a bad impression. Should you ask someone to edit your statement, not for content, but for grammar and style? There's nothing wrong with getting another's suggestions about the best way to phrase an idea or convey a point. However, do not go so far as to have someone else rewrite the essay for you. Although the reader may not know that you were assisted in writing your essay, remember that the LSAT, GMAT, GRE, and MCAT all include writing samples. It is easy enough for the reader to corroborate your writing style and level of sophistication with these other samples. Of course the entrance-exam essays are written under severe time pressure and will not truly reflect your writing ability. Still, if the reader sees an entrance-exam essay that suggests limited command of the language alongside a brilliantly crafted personal statement, the reader will have good reason to doubt that the same person wrote both.

Perhaps English is your second language and your English writing skills are still developing. If you are applying for admission to a program in which verbal skills are not important, you will probably not jeopardize your chances of admission by receiving substantial assistance in writing your essay. In fact, the school would probably appreciate your efforts and make a more informed decision if your statement is intelligible and reasonably communicative as to your academic goals. In this event, it is advisable to acknowledge in the essay that you received assistance; the reader will appreciate your candor, which will no doubt work in your favor.

SUBMITTING SUPPLEMENTAL MATERIALS

What about submitting additional materials that supplement, illustrate, or support your personal statement? It would seem that samples of your academic work that evidence your scholarship, intellect, and writing ability would help any admissions committee make a more informed decision about your application. Nevertheless, unless they are specifically requested by the school, theses, dissertations, books, articles, or other papers you submit are generally not read by the decision-maker(s). The same holds true for newspaper clippings, magazine articles, or other materials written *about* you or about an organization in which you have been actively involved. The schools are deluged with materials like these, and very few schools take the time to examine them and consider them in the decision-making process. This is not a universal rule, however, so if you think supplementary materials would provide the reader with an important insight about you, contact the individual schools to determine their policies.

As for submitting samples of your work *other than writing*: if your hobby or previous career involved photography or some other art form, or if you are currently an entrepreneur in the business of producing a particular product, you may want the admissions committee to see a sample of your work. Do not think for a minute, however, that your work can take the place of a written personal statement. In fact, be forewarned that unless the sample relates directly to the personal statement itself, its submission may call into question your judgment and give the school reason to deny your application.

[Applications to programs in the arts are obvious exceptions to the foregoing advice. Portfolios are customarily required for admission to graduate programs in the fine arts and performing arts.]

THE TOP 10 DO'S AND DON'TS FOR WRITING PERSONAL STATEMENTS

The following checklists recapitulate the main points from Part 1 so far. Observe these ten DO's and ten DON'Ts, and you can rest assured that your personal statement will make a distinctly positive impression.

✎ TOP 10 RULES TO WRITE BY

1. DO strive for depth rather than breadth: narrow your focus to one or two themes, ideas, or experiences.

2. DO tell the reader what no other applicant will honestly be able to say.

3. DO provide the reader with insight into what drives you—i.e., what makes you "tick."

4. DO be yourself rather than pretending to be the "ideal" applicant.

5. DO get creative and imaginative, particularly in your opening remarks.

6. DO address the particular school's unique features that attract you.

7. DO focus on the affirmative in the personal statement itself; consider an addendum to explain deficiencies or blemishes.

8. DO evaluate your experiences rather than merely recounting them.

9. DO enlist others to proofread your essay for grammar, syntax, punctuation, word usage, and style.

10. DO use a highly readable typeface with conventional spacing and margins (on paper-based applications).

✎ TOP 10 PERSONAL-STATEMENT PITFALLS

1. DON'T submit an expository resume; avoid merely repeating information already provided elsewhere in your application.

2. DON'T complain or whine about the "system" or about your circumstances in life; however, constructive criticism is fine as long as it relates directly to your career goals.

3. DON'T get on a soapbox and preach to the reader; while expressing your values and opinions is fine, avoid coming across as fanatical or extreme.

4. DON'T talk about money as a motivating factor in your plans for the future.

5. DON'T discuss your minority status or disadvantaged background unless you have a compelling and unique story that relates directly to it.

6. DON'T remind the school of its ranking among the various programs of its type.

7. DON'T waste your personal statement opportunity with a hackneyed introduction or conclusion.

8. DON'T use a gimmicky style or format.

9. DON'T submit supplemental materials unless the school requests them.

10. DON'T get the name of the school wrong.

PERSONAL STATEMENTS AND MEDICAL SCHOOL APPLICATIONS

Most medical schools require personal statements at two different steps in the application process: (1) the initial AMCAS application and (2) the supplemental (or secondary) application. Each step includes some unique aspects, as discussed below.

✎ THE AMCAS "PERSONAL COMMENTS" ESSAY

About 115 medical schools participate in AMCAS (American Medical College Application Service), a centralized application service created by medical-school admissions officers to simplify and standardize the medical-school application process. Part 3 of the AMCAS application requires an essay that the instructions refer to as "Personal Comments."

This essay is extremely open-ended. The instructions suggest that you consider discussing any of the following:

- Your reasons for selecting the field of medicine

- Your motivation to learn more about medicine

- Special hardships, challenges, or obstacles that may have influenced your educational pursuits

- Significant fluctuations in your academic record that are not explained elsewhere in your application.

- Anything else you want medical schools to know about you that hasn't been disclosed in another part of the application

The "Personal Comments" essay must be no more than 5,300 characters in length (equivalent to approximately one full page).

Since the same AMCAS application is sent by AMCAS to every school to which you apply, it is obviously inappropriate to discuss in this application your reasons for applying to any *particular* school. As a result, you may wonder whether AMCAS essays are actually read by the schools, especially considering that some participating schools may receive as many as 10,000 AMCAS applications during one year! The fact is that your AMCAS essay will not necessarily be read at every school that *receives* your AMCAS application, but it will be read at every school that considers you a viable candidate for admission.

✎ "SUPPLEMENTAL" OR "SECONDARY" APPLICATION ESSAYS

In addition to the AMCAS application, many schools require a *supplemental* or *secondary* application that includes a series of short-essay questions. The questions typically deal with such topics as extracurricular activities, employment, and why the applicant is interested in this particular school. Secondary applications do not typically call for open-ended personal statements. The questions are usually more specific. The number of questions included in secondary applications varies, but 8 to 10 is average. A minority of AMCAS schools allow applicants to submit an additional personal statement along with their secondary applications. (Contact the schools directly beforehand to determine their policies.)

Medical schools that do not participate in AMCAS require applicants to respond by written essay to the school's own specific questions and will usually require an open-ended personal statement. Curiously, secondary applications from AMCAS schools often include just as many or more essay questions than applications from non-participating schools.

✎ APPLYING TO LAW SCHOOLS VIA THE LSAC WEB SITE

An efficient way to complete and submit electronic applications to multiple law schools is through the Web site of the Law School Admission Council (www.lsac.org). At the LSAC site you can fill in a form with information common to all applications, then select the schools to which you want to apply, and the information is automatically inserted into the proper fields in each school's application. Some data fields, including those for personal statements, you'll need to complete separately for each application. You'll save your application information on LSAC's secure central database, so you can access it any time. Once you've completed your applications, you can print them out and mail them to the law schools yourself, or you can transmit them electronically to the schools via LSAC's electronic application clearinghouse. All 184 ABA-approved law schools accept applications electronically via LSAC.

NOTE: LSAC also offers a CD-ROM with the same features as the Web-based product described above. Neither version is free; and the fee you'll pay for either one is in addition to the application fees that the law schools assess.

THE AMCAS APPLICATION FORM (FOR MEDICAL-SCHOOL ADMISSION) AT THE AAMC WEB SITE

If you're applying to one or more of the approximately 115 medical schools participating in AMCAS (American Medical College Application Service), you must first complete and submit to AMCAS the official AMCAS application form—via the AMCAS area of the AAMC (American Association of Medical Colleges) Web site (www.aamc.org). The electronic application includes a field for the "Personal Comments" essay. AMCAS assembles your completed application file, verifies it, and forwards the application (which includes your essays) to your designated medical schools.

NOTE: Before completing the "Personal Comments" portion of the AMCAS application form, be sure to read carefully the instructions for this portion, which provide specific information about how to format—and *not* to format—your essay.

PART 2

Recommendation Letters and In-Person Interviews

As if writing personal statements for all of your applications were not enough, you will also have to arrange for recommendation letters and, in many cases, in-person interviews. Don't panic. In this part, you will learn all about these aspects of the admissions process—everything from selecting and approaching potential recommenders to making your best impression at interviews. Additional insights from the admissions experts are available in Part 4.

RECOMMENDATION LETTERS

Recommendation letters (commonly referred to in the admissions business as "rec letters") play an important role in the admissions process by providing an objective and candid evaluation of the applicant from a disinterested third party. Most schools require anywhere from one to three letters, although some schools make recommendation letters optional.

✎ WHAT THE SCHOOLS WANT TO KNOW FROM YOUR RECOMMENDERS

Recommendation forms vary somewhat among the schools in terms of format as well as specificity and number of questions. Some recommendation forms are very open-ended, simply asking the recommender to evaluate the applicant's qualifications in a separate letter. More common, however, is the type of form that includes perhaps four to six questions, each calling for a brief response written directly on the form. The following is a representative sampling of the kinds of questions appearing on recommendation forms:

Very Common

"How long have you known the applicant?"

"What is the nature of your relationship with the applicant?"

"Comment on the applicant's potential for intellectual and professional growth."

"How would you compare the applicant's intellectual abilities, character, and personality relative to other students whom you have also recommended for admission to this school?"

"Does the applicant have any unique skills or talents that you have observed?"

"In your observation, how would you assess the applicant's character and integrity?"

Somewhat Common

"What are the candidate's greatest strengths?"

"In which areas could the applicant most benefit from further growth and improvement?"

"Is there anything unusual or unique about the applicant that would help contribute to the diversity of our student body?"

"Do you consider the applicant's achievements to be truly reflective of his/her ability? Explain."

"In your estimation, has the applicant given careful consideration to his/her commitment to graduate study as well as to a subsequent career?"

Less Common

"In your observation, how has the applicant reacted under stress, academic or otherwise?"

"How would you assess the applicant's social skills and judgment of people?"

"If the applicant's first language is not English, how well does he or she read, write, and speak English?"

"Discuss the applicant's insight into his or her own assets and liabilities."

"Has the applicant demonstrated a commitment to improving the lives of others? If so, explain."

"Do you consider the applicant to be emotionally stable and in good health?"

More Common for Law-School Admissions Than for Other Programs

"Comment on the applicant's capacity for original thought."

"What is your assessment of the applicant's ability to analyze and assess information critically?"

More Common for Business-School Admissions Than for Other Programs

"Discuss the applicant's ability and willingness to work in a team environment."

"How would you evaluate the applicant's leadership qualities?"

✎ THE CHECKBOX OR "GRID" APPROACH

Many schools provide a form that allows the recommender to rate the applicant according to different criteria by checking the appropriate response—e.g., excellent, above average, etc. (such forms typically include a series of essay questions as well). Look for any of these criteria on this type of form:

analytical ability	maturity
oral communication skills	self-confidence
written communication skills	creativity
initiative	problem-solving skills
intelligence	sensitivity to others
intellectual curiosity	breadth of knowledge
integrity	overall rating
interpersonal skills	

On business-school recommendation forms, also look for these criteria:

leadership ability/potential
decisiveness
organizational ability
ability to work with others
initiative/motivation/drive
managerial potential
career-advancement potential

clarity of career goals
flexibility
respect accorded by management
respect accorded by peers
quantitative skills
sense of humor/perspective

✎ SELECTING YOUR RECOMMENDERS

Generally speaking, law schools, medical schools, and graduate programs prefer *academic* recommendations, while business schools prefer *work-related* recommendations. (For more details, read the admissions officials' comments in Part 4 of this book.) These are not hard-and-fast rules, however. There is nothing wrong per se with submitting both academic and employment-related recommendations. What is most important is that your letters are from people who know you well and who can make informed comments about the various criteria listed on pages 31–32. That person might be a teacher, teacher's assistant, school administrator, employer, supervisor, or co-worker. Examine the recommendation forms from the schools that interest you for clues about whom to ask for letters. What questions are posed? If a grid or check-box is included, what criteria are listed? Who knows you and would best be able to respond to this particular form?

DO NOT submit *character* references from family, friends, influential alumni, or public figures. The recommender's notoriety or stature is not important. Believe it or not, schools see many recommendation letters from high-ranking political figures. Unless the recommender knows you well enough to respond to the questions asked, such a letter won't help you.

✎ APPROACHING AND ASSISTING POTENTIAL RECOMMENDERS

Assuming the recommender can honestly write a generally positive letter on your behalf, do not be the least bit hesitant to approach him or her for a recommendation—especially a college professor since one of the implicit job duties of instructors is to write recommendation letters for students. Don't be concerned that you are imposing when you request a recommendation letter; just provide the individual with all the help you can so he or she can do the job.

Consider making an appointment to discuss your request (perhaps during office hours for professors). Wining and dining (or some other form of wheel greasing) your potential recommender is inappropriate unless you are already well-acquainted personally. More students err in the other direction by simply handing their recommendation form to the individual and asking if he or she would be willing to fill it out. Consider arranging *two* meetings with your recommender. During the first meeting, provide him or her with your recommendation forms and copies of your personal statements. Your essays will give your recommender clues about how you wish to present yourself and to be presented to the admissions committee. As a result, the recommender's comments will be more likely to corroborate, reinforce, and complement what you have told the school yourself. Your essays will also provide a starting point for the recommender, who may have to do a bit of brainstorming to determine what to write about you. During the second meeting, the recommender can comment on the particular themes that you brought up in your essays and ask any questions that may have occurred to him or her between the two meetings.

Recommenders will appreciate your taking more time and making these additional efforts to assist them in writing meaningful and positive letters. A word of caution, however: don't take the idea of assisting the recommender too far. Do not write a draft of the letter for the recommender, even if he or she requests it. Just as experienced admissions officials have an uncanny sense for recognizing a personal statement that was written by someone other than the applicant, they can also spot a recommendation letter that was written by the applicant and signed by a nominal recommender. If your letters (or your personal statement) arouse suspicion, the school might follow up on the matter by contacting your recommender. The end result of such investigation may be an automatic denial of admission.

✎ UNDERGRADUATE PLACEMENT FILES AND CREDENTIAL SERVICES

At many undergraduate institutions (particularly four-year colleges), students can compile a collection of academic reference letters by asking faculty members (and others, such as administrators and teaching assistants) to write letters of reference on the student's behalf. These are then kept on file with the school's placement office or other appropriate department. Such letters are almost always acceptable for the purpose of graduate- and professional-school applications even though the recommender is not addressing any particular school.

According to admissions officials, there are advantages as well as disadvantages to using these letters in applying for graduate study. One view is that, since the recommender's relationship with the applicant was "current" when the letter was written, the letter is more likely to be meaningful than one written years later in response to a request by a former student who is now applying for graduate study. Moreover, the authenticity of such letters is rarely questionable.

On the other hand, because such letters could have been written years ago, many admissions officials (particularly those at graduate business schools) question the usefulness of these letters in assessing the applicant's current interests and abilities. Also, these letters do not allow the recommender to address the particular school to which the student is applying. For example, the admissions committee may want to know how the recommender would rank the applicant among others whom the recommender knows and who have applied to and/or gained admission to the particular school. This sort of information cannot be obtained from a placement-file reference letter.

✎ IF THE SCHOOL DOES NOT REQUIRE RECOMMENDATION LETTERS

If a school does not require recommendation letters, you should generally submit at least one or two anyway, just because almost all other applicants will do so. If you doubt this advice, read the interviews later in this book. Where letters are optional, the decision-makers will not automatically look either favorably or unfavorably on your decision to submit or not submit letters. If you think your recommenders will help your cause, submit the letters; otherwise, don't.

✎ SUBMITTING FEWER OR MORE LETTERS THAN REQUIRED

It is unlikely that a school will refuse to receive and retain in your file any recommendation letter just because your file already includes a certain number of letters. Also, as a general rule, additional letters beyond the minimum required number will be read and considered, but only up to a point—a mass mailing, for example, would probably work against you. If you submit *fewer* letters than the minimum number required by the school, you probably have some explaining to do. Some schools explicitly provide in their application the opportunity for you to explain such deficiencies. Otherwise, consider providing an explanation as an addendum to your personal statement.

✎ "SEALED" RECOMMENDATION LETTERS

A "sealed" recommendation letter is one that is enclosed in an envelope with a seal affixed to the flap. Because it is impossible to tamper with the letter without breaking the seal, a "sealed" recommendation letter assures the school that the letter has not been altered or replaced. To ensure the authenticity of the seal itself, a college or university sending a recommendation letter will use its own unique seal that cannot be readily duplicated. As an additional precautionary measure, the seal itself can be signed by an official at the institution or by the recommender; in fact, this additional precaution may be *required* by the school to which the applicant is applying. This additional measure is particularly important when the recommender is not affiliated with an organization that has a distinctive seal and must resort to using a standard seal from a stationery store; of course there is no assurance against forgery in such cases.

✎ WAIVING YOUR RIGHT OF ACCESS TO RECOMMENDATION LETTERS

Recommendation forms are included in applications to most schools. Almost invariably, the form includes a *waiver* for the applicant to sign at his or her option. The waiver will probably say something like this:

> "Sign below if you wish to waive your right of access to the recommendation letter. If you do not sign, you will reserve your right of access after your matriculation to [our school]. . . ."

> ". . . I waive any right to access to this recommendation, including any accompanying comments and letters, as completed." [applicant's signature]

Don't assume that by waiving access to a recommendation letter you cannot ask your recommender to share the contents of the letter with you.

The *recommender* is not obligated to confidentiality in any way. By signing a waiver, you forgo any right to compel the *school* to produce the letter upon your matriculation (enrollment). While you won't be penalized *per se* for not waiving access to a letter, such a letter might not carry as much weight—the school might wonder whether the recommender was as forthright and objective as he or she otherwise would have been.

Is there any practical reason for *not* signing a waiver? Under certain circumstances, yes. Suppose that after matriculating at a particular school (which received recommendation letters on your behalf), you decide to apply for admission to another program at some other school, and recommendation letters are required for admission to the second school as well. Should you contact the individual who submitted a letter on your behalf to the first school about submitting another letter? In answering this question, it would help if you knew what the recommender said about you in the letter to the first school. If you did not sign a waiver, you would retain the right of access to that letter from the first school.

✎ SUBMITTING A "DEAN'S CERTIFICATION"

In addition to recommendation letters, some schools require a "Dean's Certification." If required, an appropriate form will be included in the application materials. The form must be completed by the academic dean of your undergraduate institution. By requiring a Dean's Certification, the school is verifying your undergraduate record as well as fishing for additional information about you that you and your recommenders may not have disclosed, particularly *negative* information (e.g., disciplinary action, criminal record, or other negative evidence about your academic or personal integrity and character). Of course, the Dean's Certification also gives the dean an opportunity to provide positive information about you. In most cases, however, the academic dean will not be personally acquainted with the applicant, or not well enough to offer personal comments. If your academic dean does not know or remember you, be assured that this will not work to your disadvantage in the admissions process; you are in the same position as most other applicants. (In fact, it is more likely to work to your advantage since academic deans are more likely to remember "problem" students.)

✎ COMMITTEE LETTERS FOR MEDICAL-SCHOOL APPLICANTS

Unique to the medical-school admissions process is the use of a "committee letter" of recommendation. Many schools require a committee of faculty and advisers at the applicant's undergraduate institution to submit a single letter on the applicant's behalf in lieu of separate individual letters. For schools that do not require a committee letter, the applicant should consider submitting one anyway, and possibly individual letters as well from people other than those participating in the committee letter.

IN-PERSON INTERVIEWS

In-person interviews afford applicants a chance to sell themselves and allow the schools to scrutinize applicants more closely to ensure that those admitted have a sufficient level of maturity, stability, and commitment to succeed in graduate school and in their chosen profession. Interviews also give schools further down in the "pecking order" an opportunity to woo well-qualified candidates away from higher-ranked schools. Nearly all medical schools require interviews. Many business schools conduct interviews for at least some applicants. For most law schools, however, the applicant's personal statement serves as a substitute for an in-person interview, although the trend among all schools (graduate and professional programs) is toward conducting more interviews to avoid over-quantification of the admissions process. The following information should respond to many of your concerns about this important aspect of the admissions process.

✎ ARRANGING FOR AN INTERVIEW

Perhaps you are concerned about *whether* or *when* you should interview or about the proper protocol and procedures for inquiring about interviews and scheduling an interview. These issues are examined below.

Is There Any Advantage to Interviewing Either Early or Late in the Season?

Many applicants interview at a few schools that are low on their priority list to gain some experience so that they are more comfortable during the interviews that are most important to them. There's nothing wrong with this strategy. Keep in mind, however, that some schools continue to interview qualified applicants even *after* all available first-year seats have been filled. (Positions for joint-degree applicants fill especially early.) So don't jeopardize your chances of admission by scheduling an interview too late in the season.

Responding to an Invitation to Interview at Your Option

Perhaps you have just received a letter from one of the schools to which you have applied inviting you to an interview at your option. Does this mean that you are a "borderline" applicant? Would you undermine your chances of admission if you decline? An invitation for an interview at your option does not mean *per se* that you are a borderline applicant. Some schools extend invitations to *all* applicants whom they are considering admitting. Other schools extend invitations more selectively. Perhaps you are deficient in one particular respect but otherwise you are a well-qualified candidate. The school might be extending an invitation to you in order to find out more about that deficiency to determine whether it should be overlooked. Or perhaps the admissions committee wants to follow up on something interesting in your application. Or perhaps you truly are a borderline applicant, and they cannot distinguish meaningfully between you and another applicant without an interview.

Except for medical schools, no school will *automatically* deny you because you decline an invitation for an interview. However, you should be aware that declining an invitation may hurt your chances of admission. If the school is seeking more information about you so that it can choose between you and another candidate, all else being equal, the school will probably admit the applicant with whom it is more familiar. Whether you accept an invitation for an interview is really a judgment call on your part. How would you assess your chances of admission based upon what the school already knows about you?

Requesting an Interview When an Invitation Has Not Been Extended

Some schools provide for interviews upon request by the applicant. This is more common among schools with a relatively small applicant pool and among schools that are not ranked with the highest. Review the application materials to determine the school's interview policy. If the literature clearly states that the school does NOT conduct evaluative interviews, do not ask for one. If a school were to make an exception for one applicant and ultimately admit that applicant, then all applicants who were denied might legitimately claim that the process is unfair.

Dropping In for an Impromptu Interview

Perhaps you are considering "dropping by" the school or making an appointment for a tour or informational interview, hoping to make a good impression and score some points while you're there. Is this a good idea? Definitely not, unless the school knows and agrees ahead of time that you are visiting for the purpose of an evaluative interview. In fact, your scheme might backfire. While the schools generally make every attempt to accommodate visitors and to field appropriate questions from applicants, they look quite unfavorably upon attempts to gain an inside advantage over other applicants.

Alternative Locations for Interviewing

Perhaps you cannot take time away from your job or other commitments. Check with the school to see if a telephone interview is possible. Although a face-to-face encounter is always most telling, a great deal of what the school is seeking by way of the interview can also be obtained over the telephone. Another option is video conferencing, which is quickly becoming a viable means of conducting interviews. Check with the school to see if it has this capability. Many schools employ field representatives who are either full-time admissions officers or interested alumni to go to the applicant to conduct the interview. (Remember the movie *Risky Business*?) Some schools send representatives to selected undergraduate institutions to interview students. These interviews are usually quite brief (perhaps 20 or 30 minutes), however, and are generally conducted prior to admissions "season" (i.e., before the school reviews and evaluates applications).

Reimbursement for Travel Expenses

If you cannot afford the expense of traveling to the school just for an interview, check with the school to see if you can be reimbursed for some or all of your travel expenses. Policies vary among the schools. While most schools do not reimburse for such expenses, some schools are more flexible and will consider requests for financial assistance on a case-by-case basis. Some will bring in any ethnic or racial minority applicant entirely at the school's expense. A few schools provide a credit against tuition expenses if and when the candidate is admitted and matriculates.

Determining Your Interviewer(s) in Advance

Can you find out in advance which faculty member(s) will interview you or request that a particular faculty member conduct the interview? Generally not. However, if you are a Ph.D. or joint-degree applicant, you *may* have more control over the situation. If you identify in your application particular faculty members who are doing research in your area(s) of interest, there is a good chance that you will interview with those faculty members. Some schools even allow Ph.D. applicants to select their interviewer.

✎ INTERVIEW FORMAT AND DRESS CODE

Schools vary widely in their interview formats. You may meet only with one or two current students for less than an hour. Or you might spend an entire afternoon talking with various faculty, students, and admissions officials, either one at a time or in groups. Be prepared as to what to expect by checking with the school beforehand. Expect to interview separately (although panel interviews are not unheard of, especially at medical schools) with at least one current student and at least one faculty member. Each interview may be an hour long. At many schools, you will also join other applicants who are interviewing that day in a tour of the facilities. A half- or full-day program will probably include lunch with other interviewees and current students. [NOTE: At medical schools, joint-degree (M.D./Ph.D., for example) applicants can expect a two-day itinerary.]

Schools do not generally impose dress codes. They are not judging you based upon your clothing tastes or budget. Suits and ties are optional, even for many business school applicants. However, don't dress too casually; sweats or other athletic apparel are inappropriate and may "turn off" the interviewer. It's best to leave the jeans at home as well.

✎ WHAT TO EXPECT DURING THE INTERVIEW

First of all, you should be prepared to elaborate upon, explain, justify, confirm, and corroborate any and all information included in your application. The interviewer will look at your essays in particular as a jumping-off point for his or her questions. This is not to say that all interviewers read your file before your interview. At some schools, expect "blind" interviews in which the interviewer reviews your file for the first time *during* the interview. Rest assured that interviews are *not* conducted for the purpose of determining your level of knowledge in an academic field. The schools will look at your undergraduate record and recommendation letters to gauge this.

Some interviewers are very casual in their interviewing approach, simply inviting you in an open-ended fashion to talk about yourself, your background, your goals, and what you think you can contribute to the school. At the other extreme, some interviewers rake their interview subjects over the coals by asking them very pointed, difficult questions.

Questions might be designed to test your level of seriousness about graduate study and the career that you wish to pursue. Other questions might be designed simply to gauge your maturity, poise, "people" skills, character, integrity, sensitivity, commitment, seriousness, and so forth. Also expect questions that force you to take a position on a controversial subject or ask you to resolve an ethical dilemma. In responding to sensitive questions, keep in mind that there is no correct answer. The interviewer is really trying to ascertain whether you are a clear and independent thinker who has the poise and self-confidence to assert yourself in a pressured situation. Although the interviewers will respect and admire your firm and well-reasoned opinions on controversial issues, avoid coming across as an extremist, fanatic, or radical (even if you are). In taking an extreme or emotional position on certain issues, you may give the interviewer reason to question your ability to see all sides of an issue as well as your emotional stability.

Certain questions may be highly personal, probing, and potentially embarrassing (especially during medical-school interviews, since medical professionals must be comfortable with the most intimate and personal aspects of the human experience). Finally, be forewarned that interviewers sometimes venture over the line of what you might think is acceptable demeanor and subject matter for an admissions interview. You may have heard stories about interviewers' embarrassing remarks or off-color jokes. This is the exception, not the rule. Nevertheless, be prepared for anything, and keep your poise and sense of humor throughout.

PART 3

Thirty Great Personal Statements
(By Successful Applicants)

Okay, you now know a lot more about how to write an effective personal statement. It would sure help, though, to see some essays that illustrate the advice in Part 1, wouldn't it? Look no further—they're right here!

Each of the sample essays in this part is authentic—written and submitted by an applicant who was admitted with the essay. You will notice as you read the essays that they are quite diverse. There are three reasons for this. First, the applicants submitting these essays were applying to different types of schools and programs (law, business, medicine, and various graduate programs). Second, the questions to which the essays respond are different. Third, each applicant has a different idea about what to say and how to say it. Thus, the essays in this book provide a realistic cross-section of the sorts of successful essays that real people submit to real schools. Keep in mind as you read these samples that most of them are excerpts rather than complete essays and that some references to specific persons, schools, and other entities have been deleted. Otherwise, they are authentic.

DON'T EVEN THINK ABOUT COPYING THE SAMPLE ESSAYS IN THIS BOOK. They are intended to illustrate the advice and suggestions offered by admissions officials as well as to inspire you and to spark ideas of your own; but they are not for copying. By plagiarizing a sample essay from this book, you will not only violate federal copyright laws but will also jeopardize your chances for admission to the school of your choice, since many admissions officers will have read this book and will be on the lookout for application essays that resemble the ones herein.

Essays That Relate a Personal Anecdote

("A funny thing happened to me on the way to . . .")

[This applicant recounts a particular incident that gives the reader real insight into what makes her "tick." Notice, by the way, that the discussion of religion is handled in a way that is not likely to offend any reader.]

Two years ago, when I was a junior in college, I wrote a story entitled "It Came from Catholic School." My friends, fellow veterans of plaid uniforms and daily masses, liked it and encouraged me to submit it when the English department magazine made its annual call for stories. They published the story and asked me to read from it at a reading primarily devoted to student poetry.

Well, I was pretty nervous about this. The only readings I'd done before a crowd were Paul's letters to the Ephesians and the occasional Responsorial Psalm—and that wasn't *my* writing on the line. I grew more nervous as I sat there that night, listening to poem after poem on angst and ennui. I couldn't imagine how the students and faculty around me, who were all listening intently with properly contorted faces, would respond to my grotesque little girl. But I stood up and read a passage, a little shaky at first. Then I heard laughs, where I'd hoped I would, and also in places that surprised me. After the reading, people wanted to shake my hand. One woman thanked me for injecting a little levity into the proceedings. I felt satisfaction in my work as never before.

At that reading, I realized I could write things that made people laugh—not just friends who felt obligated, but complete strangers. I really liked that feeling, and it's the promise of that laughter that motivates me to continue writing. I also realized that my work wasn't frivolous, that I could influence a reader, that my characters seemed real. For the first time, I felt that I could do what I really wanted to do—write.

I look forward to progressing through a series of intimate workshops *en route* to an MFA degree at your school. The interdisciplinary nature of the program appeals to me. Although I want to concentrate on Fiction, I would like to take screenwriting electives as well. I think my humor translates well to teleplays, and I would like to explore that avenue through the comedy writing courses your school offers. I aim to develop my natural strengths—humor, voice, and dialogue—while experimenting with the genres. Because I'm generally at the mercy of my characters, I can't outline a specific writing goal. I do envision myself producing a collection of short stories featuring female protagonists. Women's issues are implicit in my writing, and I would welcome the chance to study with *[faculty name]*. My stories feature a range of women—from the precocious heroine of the aforementioned story to a "white trash" cashier—I plan to cover a still broader scope. Mainly, I'm looking to devote myself to the work. And I hope to make some people laugh along the way.

[This successful law-school applicant opened with an intriguing and captivating introductory paragraph, then continued by relating an experience that tells the reader that this person has something unique to contribute to the student body.]

I entered boot camp on June 18, 1989. That day, the Indian child who had chased cows and the American youth who had philosophized about physics died. It is written in the Bhagavad-Gita that in death, the body's attachment to materialism falls away from the soul like a worn garment. So did my delusions of grandeur slip from me.

After graduating from high school, I enlisted in the Army Reserves to help pay for college. I was promptly sent off to Basic Training. Receiving multiple kicks of the drill sergeant's boot while doing push-ups that first day in the hot sun of Fort Dix, New Jersey, I realized why it's called boot camp. For the next ten weeks, my fellow recruits and I would be rudely awakened every morning at

4:30. The day began with nonstop backbreaking exercises, euphemistically called conditioning activities. It would continue with marching, rifle firing, indoctrination, and more conditioning activities interrupted only by meals. Tired from yelling all day, at 10:00 p.m. the drill sergeant would permit us to clean our barracks and sleep. . . . Basic Training was tough, but Officer Candidate School was tougher and six times longer. For the next sixteen months, I crammed for classes, crawled through mud-pits, studied military strategy, and led training exercises. I realized I hated soldiering. . . .

Coming from an intense and diverse background, I am well prepared for law school. My military life has nurtured a high code of ethics and a heightened sense of civic duty. My study of science has forced the development of acute analytical skills and a habit of diligence. Finally, having been in the Army and at a university, I can communicate well with a wide range of people on many levels.

[This applicant successfully told about overcoming cultural disadvantage by creating an interesting short story for the reader.]

The spring quarter had just ended in my second year of college. As I sat in the airplane, waiting for it to take off, I was terrified. If man was meant to fly he would have been given wings, and since I did not have a pair of wings, flying was very uncomfortable for me. Although the excitement of backpacking through Europe slowly began to dissipate this feeling of flight anxiety, the roar of the engines and the sluggish movement towards the runway sent my fear sky high. With death impending, my thoughts turned retrospective, reviewing moments of my past and how they would affect the future that I would not have.

This was not my first flight on an airplane, so I could not explain this deathly fear of flying. My initial introduction to flying came when I was four, traveling half way across the world from South Korea to meet my new family in America. Although I was flying alone, I soon met several passengers who were happy to keep an eye on me and help me pass the time. When the flight was over, I was introduced to my new family; there were Thomas and Penny, a.k.a. Dad and Mom, and two boys and two girls, who I am proud to call brothers and sisters.

I don't know about reincarnation or anything like that, but I felt that I had known this group of people forever. It was as if I was a piece of a jigsaw puzzle; I was a piece, and combined with others, we made a nice "picture." From the first day, I gave them as much love as a person could give, and received it back tenfold. There were the usual family problems—fighting siblings and parental confrontations—but we were a great family. I never really thought that I or my family was different until we moved to a small town on the coast.

The town was predominantly filled with white, middle class people. When I arrived I was 12 and the only Asian in the entire school. It never occurred to me that I was different, but as people started to harass me about my looks, I was devastated that I did not fit in. My family gave me a lot of support, and with a lot of determination, I was soon accepted as one of the guys. These initial experiences, however, imprinted an image about the naivete of people, and how quick people are to judge a person without getting to know him first. However bad the experience was, it did make me a better person, making me more prone to give people a chance before passing judgment on them.

. . .

All I had to do was survive the airplane flight. After a few moments of turbulence and very dangerous levels of anxiety, the plane began to fly smoothly. I finally settled down as I began reviewing my makeshift plan of attack to see Europe. My life was in order, unlike the points of Europe I wanted to see, but then, who wants to follow a set plan when there is so much to see!

Essays That Admit Shortcomings

("I'm only human, after all.")

[This essay epitomizes the personal statement in the sense that it provides the reader a very personal look at the human being behind the application. It shows a great deal of thought and demonstrates the applicant's maturity and sense of perspective.]

I sat down today to write an essay which undoubtedly would have followed the same format that you have seen a thousand times before, but after tonight I don't think that would really be appropriate. I am an accomplished student. As an Environmental Resources Engineering student I am trained to think and problem solve. Consistently I am placed in leadership positions by my peers, and I have a reputation for doing work well beyond what is expected. Since my return to school five years ago, my goal has been to be known and respected by my peers solely based on a reputation for producing excellent work. On July 28, 1992 my life changed, but not my goals. I got married to the kindest, most caring woman I've ever known. For the last two and a half years spending time with her has been the single most important extracurricular activity in my life, and today I was reminded of that.

After considering attending law school for several months, I made the final decision last August. Since then, it has been at the forefront of my mind. This semester in school has been a very demanding one. I have half a dozen major design projects going on, and have been designated the group leader in three of the four group projects. I like leading the charge in my group design projects. It is especially rewarding when my peers turn to me for leadership and help when I am not officially designated as the leader. It has a very significant side effect though: loss of time.

Fortunately, budgeting time is one of my strengths. I am in class 25 hours a week, I operate a small business providing information to a power agency, I direct many efforts within my group design projects, I stay on top of my homework, attend some engineering club activities, and spend time with my wife. With 24 hours in a day, six lost to sleep, and countless others lost to running the household, aided by my wife, this is no small task. Lately it got a little harder.

When we were married, my wife left her friends and family in Canada and followed me down to California to an uncertain future. I had just transferred to a California state university. I had no job and only a few thousand dollars saved up from my job at the power agency. That job involved long term resource planning and policy. There was not much call for these skills in this rural area. We spent our first three weeks living in a tent. It was cold and miserable, but she stayed with me, toughing out the rain, fog, and camp stove dinners. We were ecstatic when I landed a temporary position writing a bid to the power agency for a demand-side management program. This meant we had an income and could move into an apartment. She put up with my long hours balancing school work with the new job. She let me drag her back to Canada when I received a summer job offer with a utilities company, helping to develop a new corporate policy to deal with the evolving regulatory environment they were facing. She put up with working lousy jobs, with lousy hours at gas stations and fast-food joints for another summer while I spent my days in the comfort of a climate controlled office. At the end of the summer I dragged her back to California, where she would continue to wait for her work permit so she could go to school and begin her life. It would be another year before that would materialize, during which I would drag her to and from Sacramento, subjecting her to more loneliness, waiting, and living with my parents for a summer.

Now, finally, after over two years of waiting she received her work authorization. She could get a Social Security Number, a job, and register for school. She was on the verge of beginning the path to building her own life and stop living in my shadow. All she needed was more of my time to help her on her way. Given that my time was already 100% occupied, she had a hard time getting it. Tonight, for the first time, she told me how bad I was making her feel. Every time she needed help, I was busy and made a fuss about giving up the time. As my flannel shirt was dampened by her tears, I was reminded just how much this person means to me, how much she had gone through for me, and how much I had been ignoring her lately. I felt repugnant.

My, our, future is important to me. I already have an excellent education. I will receive a degree in a growing field and have a phenomenal amount of pertinent experience for a person of 24. I want to go to law school. I especially want to attend your school. This feels right. I have seen the difference I could have the opportunity to make with a Juris Doctor. I am a student with the intellectual capacity, the real world experience, and the tenacity and courage to excel at your school. I am also aware of how precious and important life beyond school and work is. If this is what you are looking for, please give me the opportunity to perform. If it's not, don't. Either way, I come out a winner. I have my wife, and I have a future. I want my legal education to make a bigger difference than I can as an engineer, but with a strong family to draw upon I cannot help but live a successful life.

[This essay responded to a question that asked applicants to discuss a personal failure and what they learned from it. Notice how this candidate recounted a "failure" in a way that actually made him a more attractive candidate for admission.]

As a District Manager at a financial services company, my success was based on the success of my representatives. In a 100% commission and independent contractor environment, I needed to make them successful quickly or they would become discouraged and leave. I had interviewed and hired each of my Representatives so I felt acutely responsible for their fate at the company. I trained them to pass the licensing requirements, and then I helped them to learn the sales scripts and the products. The management philosophy was that we could make anyone successful with the program and skills plus effective management and motivation.

I spent all my time and effort trying to make the Representatives I managed successful. I failed. I worked three months with one Representative to pass his licensing examinations. I tutored him unrelentingly until he finally passed. I went out with him on countless appointments to try and figure out why he was not able to close sales. I even bought him some ties and white shirts. I believed that he would eventually be successful, but I was not sure how long my Branch Manager would let him stay in the office. I protected him for months, but in the end, he depleted his life savings and started falling into serious debt. He had to leave and find a more steady paying job. I think he is now selling cars. The same type of story happened over and over again. Even though we were a financial services firm, the Representatives generally left in a worse financial situation than when they joined the company.

My disappointment was that I was not able to make the Representatives successful within the confines of the program. I analyzed every aspect of the program. I kept coming back to the conclusion that the company actually came out ahead when the Representatives left. The Representatives were independent contractors so they were not paid until they obtained licensing and closed a sale. New representatives typically closed several large sales to either family members or friends. After a few more weeks they would become disillusioned at the difficulty of the program and then leave. The company would then take over the accounts. I received compensation only for my own business and from overrides from my representatives. The time spent recruiting and training was not compensated. We advertised a financial management training program, but fewer than five other people reached the District Manager stage in over three years. I have no doubts that I gave my all to my Representatives, and I have no regrets in working at that company. I learned how to sell, train, and manage. The management strategy was at each stage of the program to "throw people at the wall and see if they stuck." I now realize that even though I "stuck" through several stages and was very disappointed in not becoming a Branch Manager, I should have left much earlier since I could never have been a Branch Manager at that company.

Essays That Connect the Applicant's Past, Present, and Future

("I always knew I wanted to be a . . .")

[A tale from your childhood can pique the reader's interest along with underscoring the earnestness of your intended academic pursuits, as this essay illustrates.]

My interest in photojournalism began when I was nine years old. After a couple of years of collecting baseball picture-cards and accumulating more than ten-thousand treasured images, my interest in acquiring posed mugshots and static faces decreased, so I liquidated my assets and discovered a new hobby: reading the sports sections of my father's newspapers. I became captivated by the genuine, timely and action-packed pictures of the 1964 Phillies appearing regularly in the Philadelphia Daily News and Inquirer. A short time later, I began a nightly ritual of clipping and collecting the grainy black-and-white photos accompanying detailed descriptions of our home team's performances.

In 1979, I resumed the practice of clipping tear-sheets, when my byline started appearing under photos and short concert reviews published in several South Philadelphia community newspapers. After some success selling articles and pictures to local, small-circulation publications, I enrolled in college, determined to pursue a career in photojournalism, and became the only member of my family to graduate from an academic institution of higher education when I received a BFA in documentary photography.

Although I am extremely satisfied with my current employment as a photographer for a world-renowned eye hospital and will continue to write articles and to photograph events on a free-lance basis, I would also eventually like to teach. With my previous experience in photojournalism, travel, politics, medicine, sports and entertainment, and as the overseer of our department's medical-photography internship program, I feel that I will make a significant contribution to the learning environment.

[In responding to a question that asked the applicant to describe experiences, events, or persons that have been important in his or her development, this applicant successfully correlated his influences to his current outlook on life.]

Perhaps the most important influence that has shaped the person I am today is my upbringing in a traditional family-oriented Persian and Zoroastrian culture. My family has been an important source of support in all of the decisions I have made, and Zoroastrianism's three basic tenets—good words, good deeds, and good thoughts—have been my guiding principles in life. Not only do I try to do things for others, but I always push myself to be the best that I can be in all aspects of my life. I saw early the doors and opportunities that a good education can open up; thus, I particularly tried hard to do well in school.

Another important experience that has had a large influence on me the past few years has been college. Going from high school to college was a significant change. College required a major overhaul of my time-management techniques as the number of things to do mushroomed. In high school, I was in the honors program, with the same cohort of students in all my classes. Thus, I was exposed little to people very different from myself. College, on the other hand, is full of diversity. I have people of all backgrounds and abilities in my classes, and I have been fortunate enough to meet quite a few of them. This experience has made me more tolerant of differences. Furthermore, a variety of classes such as the Humanities Core Course, in which we specifically studied differences in race, gender, and belief systems, have liberalized my world view.

My undergraduate research has occupied a large portion of my time in college. Along with this experience have come knowledge and skills that could never be gained in the classroom. I have gained a better appreciation for the medical discoverers and discoveries of the past and the years of frustration endured and satisfaction enjoyed by scientists. I have also learned to deal better with the disappointments and frustrations that result when things do not always go as one expects them to. My research experience was also important to me in that it broadened my view of the medical field. Research permitted me to meet a few medical doctors who have clinical practices and yet are able to conduct research at the university. This has made me seriously consider combining research with a clinical practice in my own career.

From my earliest memories, I can always remember being interested in meteorology. I believe that this interest sparked my love for the outdoors, while my interest in medicine molded my desire for healthy living. As a result of these two influences, I try to follow an active exercise routine taking place mostly in the outdoors. I enjoy running and mountain biking in the local hills and mountains, along with hiking and backpacking. All of these activities have made me concerned about the environment and my place in it.

[Notice how this successful applicant avoids the expository-resume approach by focusing on two or three particular experiences and evaluating them in terms of her current outlook and educational goals. Also notice how the discussion about her children's activities, while seemingly unnecessary to make her central point, helps to bring the essay down to a more personal level.]

My first employment in a library was in a work-study project during college. My duties included some shelving and a lot of typing of catalog cards. I remember the sturdy metal stacks, with so many captivating books tempting me as I tried to reshelve all that were on the carts. Mostly I remember the typing; agonizingly laborious since I was not a skilled typist, and formatting was so important. I came to understand much about the way the cataloguing system worked, and was grateful in the years to come when I needed to locate things for my own studies . . . or for my children.

For more than fifteen years now I have been working as a volunteer for La Leche League International, a grass roots, non-profit, self-help organization supporting and promoting breastfeeding. My work for the organization has taken a number of forms over the years, but can be summed up as gathering information, both practical and technical, and using human relations skills to make it accessible to others. My experience helping women access breast-feeding information and empowering them to use that information has convinced me that information alone is not nearly as useful as information *plus* a skilled guide.

One of my greatest pleasures in recent years has been writing a regular column—"Keeping Up-to-Date"—for La Leche League's bimonthly international newsletter. Through this experience I have seen a vivid contrast between the substantive quality of information formally prepared—with the discipline and rigor of a traditional publishing and review schedule and with clear authorship—and the casual unstructured nature of electronic bulletin board postings, faxes, e-mail, and other products of newer technologies. I am practically, though peripherally, aware of some of the problems our society faces in an era when intellectual property suddenly has so many new forms. I am eager to be a well-informed participant in the discussion of intellectual participation.

This week I found myself intrigued again by cataloguing when I needed to outfit my youngest son, now twelve, with a juggler's outfit for the school play. An initial subject search for "costumes" in the OPAC system at our township library was fruitless. Only when I thought to enter "costume" without the plural "s" did the system yield all the information I needed. What frustration! This confluence of technology and information, especially as it affects accessibility, fascinates me.

The degree to which your School of Communication, Information and Library Studies openly accepts the challenge to explore and lead in the information revolution is seductive. What a serendipity that this school is practically in my backyard! The strengths and attributes I bring to your school are a caring and careful nature, proven academic excellence, experience in writing and speaking for a variety of audiences, and a practical knowledge of working with volunteers and professionals. The durability of my enthusiasm for libraries and the people who work in and love them convinces me that the Master of Library Service program is indeed the right way for me to continue my formal education.

Essays by Risk-Takers with Distinct Points of View

("I can see your school quite clearly from out here on a limb.")

[Here is a wonderfully imaginative essay that risks allowing the reader a glimpse at the applicant's playful and inventive mind.]

This personal statement has been looming over me throughout this application process. I find myself unable to overcome the seeming impossibility of this exercise. How can I convey enough of myself in two pages? I act. I sing in the shower. I occasionally reread the collection of comic books I amassed during high school. I enjoy helping people, but I do it for myself. Lately I've been dressing a little sharper. I play hockey whenever I can. And I question everything, often in the hopes of effecting a change.

Which is why the law interests me. Not to work within the system, but to change the system. But to change it, you must first understand it. To understand it, you must first get accepted to Law School. Which leaves me writing impossible personal statements.

Trapped by this inelegant thought process, I decided to take a walk and hope for inspiration. While I walked, I did what I often find myself doing. I imagined that my hands suddenly had energy, and that I could throw globs of fire or light from them. Whoosh. Whoosh. "Strange," you must be thinking, as you consider forwarding my application to the nearest psychiatric unit. I do this a lot while walking around—I'm still waiting for my latent superpowers to kick in. Sometimes walking to class, I break into a run for no reason, excepting that I feel like I would be there already if I were flying. I wait to be lifted in the air. I have spent entire class periods trying to push a pen across a paper with my mind. I assume this is not normal. But these thoughts kept coming back, the more I tried to answer the question: "Who am I?"

I took it a step further. I have been surrounded by extraordinary people all my life. From a family of brilliant type A personalities, I came out a type B: more relaxed and easygoing. Moreover, I was inclined to question the process of achievement first, rather than simply reaching the next level. My family would patiently explain to me why they thought it was important to excel in education, to play hockey, to keep writing. When I eventually understood, I would excel.

I attended an east-coast "prep" school—amongst the brighter members of the Rockefeller and Pillsbury clans. Then to an Ivy League college, where I found a far more diverse spectrum of brilliance. Once again I found that I allowed myself to lose sight of the goals and question the process itself. Why was there an English major? Why the rigid professionalism? Why were whole periods of literature only dealt with from a feminist viewpoint, or a conservative canonical viewpoint. My senior thesis became a debate on the origins of literary study. My peers in the English department were shocked. Not (horrors) Relevance!

Finally, I find myself here, amongst the best and brightest—the law school applicant pool. I don't find it humbling or scary; I've dealt with you all my life. But I yearn to somehow be exceptional, in a way that would even impress myself.

And so I finally came up with a symbol, one that makes a personal statement. I stand before you, with palms facing up. And flames sprout from my hands in an elegant plume. And slowly the flames take a shape, twisting, curling and licking each other until they form a rose of red, green, and white flames, the stem just barely touching my fingertips. And this is my totem: the flames would be my passion, and my desire to effect a change—the rose would be a symbol of my romantic life vision. Maybe. Mostly I'd just like to do it.

[This applicant's lively and unique approach to the "why I want to be a lawyer" essay captures the reader's interest. Notice that the applicant discusses her religious beliefs sensitively, without proselytizing or preaching.]

My interest in the law began with donuts. As a child, I developed early persuasive skills during family disagreements on how to divide boxes of the treats. My parents belonged to the "biggest people deserve the most donuts" school of thought; while as the youngest family member, I was a devout believer in the "one person, one donut" principle. The debates were often cutthroat, but when it came to donut distribution, I sought justice at any cost.

As my family grew older and more health-conscious we stopped eating donuts, and for many years I forgot our childhood debates. However, some recent life decisions have brought to mind those early explorations of justice. When I first arrived at the American International School of Rotterdam, I quickly learned that my colleagues were a diverse and talented group of people. Unsure of how to establish my own place among them, I tried phrases that had always worked to impress college friends. "When I work for the UN . . . ," I told the second grade teacher, and she answered with an erudite discussion of the problems she faced as a consultant for that organization. "When I'm in law school . . . ," I told the kindergarten teacher, only to hear about his own experiences in law school. By the time I discovered that even many grade-school students were better travelled than I, I learned to keep my mouth shut!

Living alone in a new country, removed from familiar personal and cultural clues to my identity and faced with these extraordinary co-workers, I started to feel meaningless. How, I wondered, could I possibly make a difference in a place as vast as our planet? To my own surprise, I found that answer at church. Although I was raised in the Bahá'í Faith, I have only recently understood the essential place that religion plays in my identity. Bahá'í social beliefs include the need to work against extreme poverty, nationalism, and prejudice; and I now realize that I cannot hold those beliefs without doing something about them. My identity rests on these convictions; I cannot see the need for help and just move on. I have to help; it's who I am.

The lessons I've learned from my international colleagues have channeled my desire for service into the field of international development. I still wish to fight the "'Biggest Get the Most' Theory of Donut Distribution," but now on an international scale.

[By suggesting his political affiliations and leanings without going so far as to impose his viewpoints on the reader, this applicant demonstrates that you can reveal your ideology in a way that any reader will respect.]

As I write this statement, Governor Mario Cuomo makes preparations to vacate the Executive Mansion in Albany, New York, after New Yorkers rejected his appeal for another term. As for me, Mario Cuomo is still a hero. He has truly lived the "American Dream." Mario, the son of first-generation Italian immigrants, rose from the poor neighborhoods of Queens to become one of the most powerful men not only in New York state but also the United States. He is respected not only for his political savvy and great oratorical skills but also as one of the greatest legal minds in the country. He is the reason I trust my hard work, dedication, and perseverance will pay.

Public policy has always appealed to me. My proudest political achievement was the successful organization of the "Register to Vote" rally at SUNY-Buffalo, which was attended by actor William Baldwin and Robert Kennedy, Jr. to campaign in support of Governor Cuomo. Also, as part of my job with the College Democrats, I have written a number of letters and opinion editorials in several Western New York newspapers; some of my letters have also been printed in News India-Times, India Abroad, and in New York magazine.

I promote my passion for writing and politics as the Cultural Affairs Editor of the largest student-run newspaper in New York state. In this position, I have taken on the many challenges that had long been avoided or pushed to the back-burner. Through my efforts, the paper presented a series of articles titled "The Diverse Spectrum," which brought out a number of race-related issues which had been previously avoided because of their controversial nature. As expected, a lot of healthy debate ensued. In addition to being a desk editor, I was granted a bi-weekly column to comment on American politics. This year, I have been hired to write weekly political columns under "Leaning Right." This is the first time in almost a decade that a student has had his own weekly political column. Two months ago, I expanded my journalistic portfolio by accepting the position of co-host on "Voices of the People," a political call-in radio show originating from the city of Niagara Falls.

Coming from a family where I am the oldest male member, I have been forced into early maturity. I realize the value of success. As a role-model to my younger siblings, it becomes imperative for me to be a positive example. My grandfather used to say, "Don't just do it; do it right." I have always tried to practice this sound advice.

Essays by Applicants Clearly Focused on Goals

("Generally speaking, my plans are quite specific.")

[In this Statement of Purpose, the applicant appears clearly focused on his research interests while maintaining flexibility in terms of his longer-term plans. Notice also how he deftly refers to particular research and work experience without resorting to the overused expository-resume approach.]

I now prepare to become more than just a professional in the field of history, but in fact a professional historian. Although my work has introduced me to other historical eras in U.S. history (including late colonial, mid-nineteenth century, and modern political history), the period of nation-forming during the early nineteenth-century has most intrigued me recently. I wonder about such things as the cultural interaction between Western and urban settings; the limits of legal institutions in a developing nation; and the significance of information to early economic, social, and political trends. The faculty at your school seems well endowed with resources to address such questions, including particularly Professor *[faculty name]* (with whom I have corresponded) and Professors *[faculty names]*. With a strong cadre of advisors, I expect to become a solid historical researcher and a partner in new directions in the field. My eclectic background in both historical work and computer technology will help me not only to do good research, but to be more aware of the emerging ideas, standards, and movements of the profession.

My background and proven abilities have led me to history with a clear purpose. I intend first and foremost to become involved in the intellectual exchange of recognized historians, helping to refine existing paradigms and to challenge worn historiographical beliefs. In addition, however, I dedicate myself to a career of writing, teaching, and presenting our history for a wider audience, touching people who rarely may consider history an instructive force for life. By thus combining careful research techniques (gathered through experience at the Smithsonian and Holy Cross archives) with an attractive style of presentation (practiced at both the Buffalo Bill Museum and Colorado Timberline Academy), I hope as well to offer the American historical experience in a manner that is genuine and meaningful on many levels, for diverse audiences. Indeed, if this truly is the work of a historian, I believe that not only am I prepared to do so, but in fact I may have already begun.

[In this Statement of Purpose, the applicant communicated clear focus and direction while remaining flexible in terms of academic pursuits and long-term career plans. The essay's technical nature is perfectly appropriate for application to a graduate program in the natural sciences.]

While my undergraduate and Master's curriculum have provided exposure to a wide variety of environmental engineering topics, I have gained extensive knowledge in relatively few areas. I have, however, found an area in which my curiosity and my ability are suitably paired. As an M.S. student I have held a research assistantship position for the last year and a half, working both at the university and at a national laboratory. The strengths of the Civil (Environmental) Engineering Department at the university, as well as those of the group at the laboratory, lie in the investigation of the fate and transport of subsurface contaminants, along with general groundwater quality and flow characteristics, and it is also within these areas that my research interests reside.

[Here the applicant describes his specific research experience.]

Although my strengths are concentrated in these areas, my curiosity is by no means limited to these topics. I believe that I have a solid foundation, but through a program of graduate study and research I hope to develop expertise in these and other related areas. One such area of interest is the remediation of contaminated groundwater and contaminant plumes by incorporating microbial processes with in situ treatment techniques. I also find the interdisciplinary relationship between environmental engineering and ecology to be of great personal interest. One particular example is the growing trend toward identifying and controlling diffuse source contamination from areas of heavy agricultural activity. The processes involved in this contamination, as well as the resultant heavy down-gradient nutrient loadings, play an extensive role in the ecological development of receiving waters and need to be understood more comprehensively. The curriculum in the Environmental Engineering Program, particularly through interactions involving the Studies in Physical & Chemical Hydrogeology program, provides an opportunity to expand my knowledge in these areas while pursuing my ambitions in the area of subterranean contaminant transport processes. Further, your graduate program would permit me to incorporate my areas of interest into an applied research project under the mentorship of the faculty in the Department of Civil and Environmental Engineering.

Ultimately, I aim to gain a faculty position at a university and to continue my involvement in innovative research in the field while directly encouraging the development of aspiring engineers, both in the classroom and laboratory. In this manner I believe I can make a significant and purposeful contribution to the scientific community while gaining a great deal of personal satisfaction.

[This personal statement conveys the applicant's clear sense of career direction and how the particular school will help the applicant meet his goals.]

My longer-term goals are in the nonprofit field. The flexibility of self-employment has given me the time and freedom to pursue my ambitions with the United Nations Association, a national nonprofit group based in New York City. For the past eleven years I have been involved with United Nations related activities, primarily educating youth about the UN through the Model UN program. I currently sit on the Executive Board of Directors of my local chapter as the treasurer. I am humbled by the dedication of our volunteers and fellow Board Members. I am also amazed at our non-business-like operations management. We still do not have a fax machine! We operate a retail operation in our community that benefits not only from a subsidized rent but also a completely volunteer labor force. And yet we barely break even.

With a more businesslike mentality we would be able to generate more money to further our educational activities. I have worked to reorganize the Chapter and retail operations to strengthen our finances and therefore our long term prospects and viability. However, my undergraduate education and mutual fund sales/management experience are insufficient for the task. The financial and management skills I learn from your school would greatly benefit our local Chapter operations and at the National level. Over the past year I have increased my involvement with UNA-USA. I currently sit on two National committees including one responsible for discussing policy direction. At your school I plan to volunteer or work Fridays at the UNA-USA office. Living in New York and obtaining a MBA from your school will give me the contacts and skills necessary to make a difference within the UN Association and with its educational mission.

I believe strongly that the key to a healthy nonprofit is business knowledge. Non-profits need to be run more like businesses in order to be competitive in the never-ending search for supporters and funding. I consider an MBA from your school as a crucial career decision and a step toward helping educate American youth about the United Nations.

[In this Statement of Purpose, the applicant clearly articulates his academic goals, corroborating them by discussing a particular undergraduate project.]

I realize that a component of graduate studies is the ability to conduct research. My formal research experience began in my early college years. There were a number of opportunities at several universities for undergraduate research, but almost all of them required citizenship or permanent residency, neither of which I had. I quickly realized that eventually I must compete with these same students when I apply for graduate school, and they would have invaluable experience which I would lack. With that motivation I began a project involving Maple (a popular computer algebra system). I concentrated on Maple as a *modeling* tool that can be incorporated into an existing course to enhance students' knowledge of mathematical concepts. My research led to two publications and a trip to Columbia University for presentation of a conference paper. I also began teaching a short course on Maple at my university, and currently I am completing a handbook entitled "Analysis of Practical Engineering Problems Using Maple" in which a software firm has expressed interest.

. . .

I would like to explore the area of biological-systems computer simulation. Medical experiments are time consuming, expensive and in some cases dangerous. Computer simulations can address some of these issues; however, biological systems pose a great challenge due to the complexity of the calculations involved. During the next few semesters, I would like to gain a deeper understanding of distributed and parallel processing, high-performance computing, medical instrumentation and bio-medical engineering. This preparation would allow me to narrow my interest to a particular area in biological simulations for a Ph.D. dissertation. I have some abstract ideas, but I need the knowledge to realize them. Your school is an ideal place for me because of the expertise it offers in both computer engineering and biomedical engineering. In particular, I hope to benefit from the works of Professors *[faculty names]*.

Essays by Applicants with Unique Life Experiences

("Like snowflakes, no two applicants are identical.")

[This applicant knew better than to hide his "misspent youth." His unique background provided just what the admissions committee welcomed—a lively story that reveals an engaging and interesting person.]

One of my biggest aspirations as a child was to become a rock star. At age 14 my band performed at my school's Valentine's Day dance. I went from being the smartest kid in the school to being the coolest. By the age of 17, I was spending my weekends in bars playing with much older musicians. At the time it didn't bother me that these older musicians all led lives that were anything but glamorous. In fact, they always seemed to be broke and were usually under the influence of drugs or alcohol (a great way of escaping reality).

It was always understood by my parents that I would attend college immediately after graduating high school. College provided me with the perfect opportunity to leave San Antonio in pursuit of stardom. Austin is well known for its music scene and just happens to have a university—the perfect choice. I was awarded a generous endowment from a private foundation that I could use at any Texas university. Within two months after starting college, I was well on my way to becoming a star. I joined a top-40 cover band and spent my weekends performing at fraternity parties and night clubs all over Texas. The band soon began performing an average of four nights a week and was earning average gross revenues in excess of $125,000. My rigorous traveling left little time for school, not that I really minded, and by the end of my second semester the University kindly informed me that I was no longer welcome as a student. Needless to say, the Foundation decided that if I wasn't going to school then I wouldn't need their money.

I spent two years as a member of the band, and during that time I lived a life that exceeded even my wildest dreams. However, the dreams of a 14-year-old boy are far different than the harsh realities of a 21-year-old adult. I came to realize that I was well on my way to becoming one of those bitter old burnouts that I used to play with when I was in high school.

I left the band and moved back to San Antonio. I began working full-time and enrolled at a junior college the following January. For the next two-and-a-half years, I worked more than forty hours per week while enrolled in nine to twelve hours per semester. Not only did my grades dramatically improve, but I also mastered the art of time management. In the past two-and-a-half years, I have learned more than just how to calculate a corporation's alternative-minimum-tax liability and how to assess control risk in an EDP environment. I have learned to appreciate the rewards of hard work and the power that comes with possessing knowledge.

[Anything unique about your upbringing might be useful to convince the admissions committee—as this applicant did—that you can offer a distinct and interesting perspective to their program.]

From my parents I learned that knowledge comes from a variety of formal and informal sources and that I will always be able to learn what I need to. I was born and grew up in Papua New Guinea, where my father was a government botanist, director of a unique equatorial botanic garden. It could have been a rather barren life. We lived in a small town, with only one restaurant and few other amenities. Local travel was limited, with only two roads leading out of town for any distance. There was an enormous richness in my home life, however. My mother was an elementary school teacher and made sure my siblings and I knew about the world around us, both close to home and overseas. She and my dad both encouraged us to learn about the culture of the local native tribes and the Chinese people who lived in town with us.

When visiting scientists from around the world came to sit on our back lawn and enjoy a beer in the cool of evening, we kids were exposed to rare and spirited discussions on a wide variety of topics.

While I was growing up books were plentiful, valued, and good quality. In an environment where there was no TV and the radio broadcast only between four and 10 p.m., reading was most definitely encouraged. I took my seventh grade classes by correspondence course, to postpone the day when I would have to go away to boarding school in Australia. One of my fondest memories is of the numerous books my mother read aloud, chapter by chapter, to my sister and me during our daily morning tea breaks that year. I learned early the importance of books for expanding horizons and providing the knowledge to undertake new activities.

[In this personal statement, the applicant focused on a particular aspect of his background and experience that conveyed to the reader that the applicant would bring something unique to the school.]

Fumbling around the inside of a makeshift magician's hat, I was deep in concentration while my mom giggled at the sight of her eldest son planning his future by drawing lots from a hat. Up to that point, my life had been decided by external forces: my parents, peer pressure, my girlfriend's parents. They all wanted me to go to school *for them.* All the while I didn't really know what I wanted to pursue. I had so many interests. My biggest problem was a fear of success. I would ask myself: "What if I decide on something, become a success, then grow unhappy because I didn't pick something else?" The magician's hat was my answer.

Each piece of paper in the hat had a word on it that symbolized one of my possible future paths: "acting," "Nordstrom," "school," "France," or "Australia." Any of these words that I should randomly choose from the hat could have a serious impact on the rest of my life. If I chose "acting," I would pursue wholeheartedly the goal of becoming a great actor—very lofty stuff. Plucking out the piece of paper with Nordstrom on it would mean that I would attempt to ascend the corporate hierarchy of the Nordstrom department store organization—could be better, could be worse. As for "school," this option was not my preferred choice at the time, but I nevertheless wanted to further my education at some point in my life—a seemingly painless course of action. What about "France"? I had relatives at the time who lived in France, and they had invited me to come live with them for as long as I liked. The lure to travel Europe was part of my interest in France as a possible choice—understandable enough. Finally, "Australia" had some of the best surf in the world—pure and simple. I had been competing in local surf contests, but I had never surfed in a major contest on foreign soil. This would be the beginning of my professional surfing career.

Nearly dizzy from closing my eyes too tight, the first word I saw when clarity finally returned was "Australia." Sticking to my guns, the next day I bought a one-way airline ticket to Australia. Upon arrival, I spent three months traveling extensively throughout the coastal continent, entering surfing contests, and marketing my clothing sponsor's new line—all the while making new friends. I had this preconceived notion that all Australians were Caucasian; boy, was I wrong! The opportunity to travel enabled me to immerse myself in the Australian experience and recognize that Australia is a highly pluralistic society. The cultures ranged from Greek, Japanese, Italian, to the Native Aborigines. The people of Australia were wonderful. My journey fed my curiosity, while getting to know the people who lived there fed my heart and mind.

After three months of traveling, the idea of being on the road was losing its appeal. I decided to go home. Many years have passed since I journeyed to the land down under. Over these years, I have either attempted or completed each one of the paths symbolized by the other pieces of paper in my makeshift magician's hat. I have ultimately learned that the only wrong choice that I could have made would have been to not put my hand into the hat at all.

Essays That Explain Why the Applicant Chose This Particular School

("If I could wish for anything, it would be to attend your school.")

[This applicant immediately engaged the reader with a witty and almost conversational style, then segued gracefully into a Statement of Purpose.]

You'd think I would have had my fill of Indiana winters. But, here I am, applying to go back, ready to dig my parka out of storage. It's not like I've been gone long enough to forget the cold, either. In some ways, I feel as if that permacloud is still hanging over me. I graduated this past May, and I think my toes just stopped tingling a couple of weeks ago. But I can deal with the winters. I can handle the Hoosiers. I don't mind if the football team loses even more games next year.

So, why come back to my alma mater? To be honest, I'll never fit the profile of the plaid-clad, legacy-bred alum who looks back on his/her undergrad experience as "da best four years of my life." I do, however, feel very grateful for the education. I majored in English and Communication, programs which complemented each other well. The time I spent in writing workshops was productive and rewarding. Also, the validation I received—the stories accepted for RE:VISIONS, the laughter and compliments at Juggler readings—inspired me to keep writing.

I feel that your program provides a nurturing and challenging environment. I aim to develop my talent, to take more risks, and to let my characters lead me, and I know I can work toward these goals in a graduate workshop setting with fewer distractions and a more committed community. I learned quite a bit from [faculty name]. He made me question certain decisions but resisted the temptation to lecture or exert too strong an influence. I regret that

I didn't get to study with [faculty name]. I think we have similar styles and concerns, Catholicism for one. A survivor of seventeen years of Catholic school, I find a wealth of material in confessionals, virgin births, and splinters of the true cross. I know I can write funny stuff, but I want to focus my wit as pointedly as she does.

Mainly, I'm looking for two years to devote to the work. I expect to be inspired by other members of the writing community and to form closer working relationships with the faculty. I'm looking forward to criticism, camaraderie, and even the cold. It builds character, so they say.

[In this Statement of Purpose, the applicant explains her reasons for applying to this particular school as well as this particular program. Her narrow focus is quite appropriate under the circumstances.]

The M.Sc. in Economic and Social History appeals to me for many reasons. First, it provides instruction in the research techniques required by history, economics, and sociology which I will need for future investigations. Second, the program is interdisciplinary, which makes it more challenging, connected, and intellectually stimulating than other similar programs. Third, it is a good way to concentrate the formal learning of research methods, the study of economic/social history, the investigation of my topic, and the writing that I enjoy, into one year. Lastly, it permits me the option to go on to the D.Phil. if I should seek to do so.

Why choose your school for this work? There are practical and professional reasons, of course. An institution like yours earns its high academic reputation by providing ready access to resources for teaching and research. My work covers British Social History from the period 1620-1760 a.d. To carry through with my study plans, I must learn research methods and materials for this phase of early modern British history. I prefer to do this in an institution located in England. The Modern History Faculty at your school has several historians with expertise in the fields, periods, and countries of interest. At the oldest university in the English-speaking world, the libraries (especially one particular library which itself dates back to my historical period), museums, and other collections provide excellent facilities for study and investigation. Your school is a short distance from London, where the Public Records Office, Institute for Historical Research, and the National Register of Archives (as well as other institutions) provide access to additional resources. All of these factors combine to make your school the best institution for my work.

There are other reasons for my choice as well. I have enjoyed my numerous trips to Britain and always look forward to each return. As a mature student, I feel the need for learning experiences based on independence and "guided self-direction." I also prefer an environment that encourages studies (at least for the D.Phil.) to be completed within three years of focused research. Your school's international reputation attracts students from all over the world, resulting in the promise of a stimulating intellectual and cultural life. The community life of a British-system university like your school will differ from the community life in American-system universities, and this feature is novel (to an American) enough to have its own attractions. The synergy that would develop among these aspects of student life is what I want for my graduate learning experience, and so I look forward to enrolling in the M.Sc. program in Modern History at your school.

Essays That Explain Deficiencies or Blemishes

("Yeah, but if you look at it another way...")

[This applicant was asked to describe significant study, travel, and employment outside of his home country. Having no such experience, he nevertheless found something useful to talk about that responded to the question.]

Other than a brief visit to England and Scotland to visit family members, I have not spent a significant amount of "developmental type" time abroad. As such, I do not have many hands-on cultural experiences to discuss. I would have liked to study abroad while in college, but was unable to primarily because of financial obligations. Those financial commitments included tending a fledgling business which I was developing during my last couple of years in college. Although the business was an international company (founded and based in Canada), my individual franchise, as successful as it was, did not develop to the point where I was able to expand into international operations.

My professional experiences at a major accounting firm have included work on several multinational clients. Those clients include a software company with international operations, a property and casualty insurer based in The Netherlands, many mutual funds with investments in international securities and a bank that provides a significant number of global custody services. Unfortunately, those professional experiences have not yet included international travel.

Despite this, I do have some interesting connections/experiences that may be interesting to the Admissions Committee. As noted above, I do have family members located throughout England and Scotland. In fact, my mother was born in England and moved with her family to the United States when she was a young child. Also interesting in this respect, I was recognized with dual citizenship by Great Britain until I turned eighteen years old. My family connections to Europe make eventual international employment more viable and attractive to me.

Another somewhat interesting connection to Europe is an experience that I had as a young child. The only significant length of time I have spent outside the United States occurred when I was one year old. My father was stationed in Germany after being drafted into the armed services. As I only lived there for about a year, I do not have significant memories of the experience. However, I do recall that we lived next door to a pig slaughterhouse! You can probably imagine the sorts of humorous stories I could tell about that experience.

[This applicant felt that his undergraduate GPA did not reflect his true potential and called this to the school's attention in a way that would leave the reader with a more positive impression.]

Discussions with administration and alumni from your school have made it clear to me that your MBA program is both an intense and academic experience. My undergraduate GPA may not indicate that I am capable of undertaking the intensity and academic challenges presented by your MBA program. I ask you to seriously consider my many other accomplishments and experiences before arriving at this conclusion.

I will admit that my GPA was not my primary concern as an undergraduate student. Without making excuses, I ask you to consider the fact that I was responsible for financing 100% of my undergraduate education. I had no choice but to work a considerable amount of my time while in school. Despite this fact, I do feel I received an excellent undergraduate education. The core curriculum and management classes contributed to the development of strong analytical and quantitative skills. From a social standpoint, my growth and experience while in college was tremendous. I feel fortunate to have developed so many friendships that I will have for the rest of my life.

[This applicant eloquently offered his own suggestion to the reader as to how to evaluate his undergraduate record.]

Some of the assets I will bring to your school cannot be reflected in formulas and numerical indices, although these numbers, when looked at more closely, are an indication of my maturity and the ability and effort I have exhibited. While reviewing my undergraduate grade point average, please consider the apparent trend, the shift of my college major, the degree GPA, and my work requirements. From the time I moved out of the house immediately following my high school graduation, I have had to support myself and my academic studies with little or no financial assistance. Although I had a job within a week after my sixteenth birthday, I was faced with fresh challenges and a brand new kind of education. I began my university courses intending to receive an English Education degree, and quickly shifted this focus when my English Literature courses challenged me and taught me more than the education curriculum. I am proud to have worked between one and three jobs simultaneously, generally demanding more than 50 hours per week, and to have simultaneously completed my Bachelor of Arts degree with course loads of up to 15 and 17 hours per semester. By comparing my work experiences to my transcript, it is evident that the more cumbersome my course load became, the better my grades were.

[This applicant's cumulative GPA suffered a bit due largely to one difficult semester. He wisely addressed this issue rather than ignoring it, recounting that semester's events in a way that would win over any school's admissions committee.]

My grades during the second semester of my freshman year of college declined because of several factors. I had been pursuing a premedical major in biology up to that time, and the spring saw me taking my first college history course which began quickly to erode my interest in pursuing a biology major. I had enjoyed and excelled in history during high school, but upon entry into college decided to take a different direction in my studies.

I made the decision to change majors after several more history courses during the following semesters, as I reconciled head and heart. That first history course—a formidable "intellectual history" oriented seminar on the French Enlightenment—was comprised of juniors, seniors and myself, the one lowly freshman. The difficulty I faced in that advanced history course and in maintaining my status in severe and involved chemistry and ecology courses affected my grades for the semester, but was a crucible out of which emerged a renewed love for and pursuit of the study of history throughout the rest of my college education.

Tackling an intellectual history seminar so early made it much easier for me to successfully complete an Honors Thesis in a later Military History seminar. My educational base is, as well, much broader because of my exploration of several different disciplines during college, including the natural sciences, archaeology, art, art history, psychology, and history. Without a tough semester to make me weigh my possibilities, I might not have continued to explore the educational options available and might have remained narrowly focused on medicine. Having temporarily performed below the expectations I had of myself, I proceeded to improve my cumulative grade point average in each successive semester.

Essays by Applicants Who Are Committed to a Cause

("Something is wrong with the world, and I'd like to try fixing it.")

[In this personal statement, the applicant tied together his heritage, his work experience, and his candid views about the health-care system to convey a well-reasoned and genuine commitment to helping others.]

My earliest impression of medicine occurred when my mother repeatedly required the assistance of physicians in dealing with her chronic migraine headaches. Her doctors were always there for her, day or night. The respect that my parents bestowed on doctors, and the doctors' ability to ease suffering, sparked a desire to one day become a physician myself. This was an ambitious goal for someone coming from a family in which no one had obtained a professional degree. However, my traditional family-oriented culture, emphasizing doing good for others, contributed to this decision to pursue a career in the medical field. Furthermore, the American individualistic spirit gave me the confidence and opportunity to undertake a challenging medical career.

I also had the chance to gain some firsthand experience in the medical profession when I volunteered for over a year in the emergency room of a regional hospital. From my volunteer experience, I learned the importance of organization and effective communication skills, and I was exposed to the diversity that exists in my community. It has also demonstrated to me why the American health-care system is the best in the world; I saw some knowledgeable minds using some very sophisticated equipment. But I also saw many ways it can be improved. For example, uninsured homeless and immigrant people would often come in, complaining of problems they had been having for a long time.

Although we would treat these people as best we could, a health-care system that intervenes in such sicknesses earlier would have minimized costs associated with treating diseases in their later stages.

As a doctor, I hope to participate in these changes in order to benefit more people than are currently being served. Doctors should be able to serve people of all different races, ages, backgrounds, and cultures. I intend to use my skills and unique experiences to achieve this vision of what I think a doctor should be.

[While in many cases one's disadvantaged background or disability may not warrant special attention in a personal statement, in some cases it does. This applicant focused on his physical disability, not to play on the reader's sympathy but as a springboard for affirming his strength of character, his resolve, and his humor.]

Of the thousands of potential students that are applying to your law school this year, what makes one person stand apart from the multitude of aspiring legal scholars? What motivates the admissions board to point to a single application and say that this individual deserves to be placed at their institution? These questions occur to me as I ponder over this statement. I must essentially sell myself to you, the reader. All of my talents, achievements and dreams become commodities in this market-place of souls. You must decide whether the package is worth purchasing; I must simply give a convincing sales pitch. Therefore, I will focus on what I think separates me from the other wares being hawked on this street: my experiences as a disabled American.

My disability has affected every possible aspect of my character. I was born with a severe form of muscular dystrophy that has rendered me a quadriplegic for nearly my entire life. As a result, I have always felt the need to prove that I am capable of achieving just as much as anyone else. My list of achievements illustrates the strong nature of my determination. I take pride in these accomplishments and feel they reflect my desire to succeed in whatever task is before me.

Despite the severe nature of my disability, I would describe myself as an independent person. During my junior year in college, I was able to move out of my parents' home and into an on-campus residence. I teach many of my own personal attendants, who are fellow students, how to best assist me. I am particularly proud of this achievement because it is not something many people in my situation are able to do. This experience has taught me to be assertive and willing to compromise, skills which will be vital in my legal career.

My unique status as a disabled college student has also put me in the position of advocate for disability issues. During my sophomore year, I was a panelist on a live, statewide PBS talk show discussing the concerns of young people with disabilities. During my junior year, I spoke at a faculty development conference regarding the needs of disabled students. I hope to continue this advocacy after I finish my legal education. It has always been my belief that the law offers the best avenue of recourse for those without a unified voice.

To become a lawyer would mean a great deal to me. It would give me the opportunity to have a significant impact on the way society grows and evolves. Hopefully, this little sales pitch of mine has convinced you that I am capable of reaching that goal. Now you must decide if you will buy or move on to the next booth.

[Rather than simply recounting academic and work experience, this applicant selected certain key experiences and evaluated them in terms of his personal development, world view, and future plans. By corroborating his vision and ideals with these particular experiences, the applicant avoids appearing naive or overly sentimental about his dedication to a cause.]

I have always been motivated toward achievement: my high school classmates voted me "Most likely to have a publishable resume." When I identify an emerging interest, my natural reaction is to pursue it actively. This instinctive drive has fueled my personal development. It has also led me to many inspiring destinations: the courtrooms of Los Angeles County; the University classrooms of Grenada; the underdeveloped economies of the Third World; and ultimately, the multilingual halls of the United Nations.

I spent my first college summer as a trained representative of the L.A. District Attorney's Victim-Witness Advocate Program, working to see that the rights of victims were as zealously protected as the rights of the accused. I enjoyed providing assistance to these under-represented citizens; however, my inability to assist adequately the numerous Spanish-speaking victims underscored the desirability, if not necessity, of being bilingual in today's world. Determined to transform my college-level Spanish into a proficient second language, I took a leave from my college and enrolled at the University of Grenada. By integrating myself into the local student community, I became immersed in the Spanish language and lifestyle. This experience sparked my fascination with other cultures. When a Moroccan classmate invited me to visit his North African homeland, I enthusiastically accepted. Our travels through this impoverished nation left me with many disturbing images: an eight-member family fixing the leaks in their canvas-covered hut; desperate children tugging on tourists' pants legs while pleading for pennies; a malnourished infant being carried off to his grave. It was a sobering introduction to the problems of the Third World.

When I returned to college in the United States, I decided to combine my newly-piqued interest in underdeveloped economies with my intensified interest in the Spanish language. I entered the Honors Program in Latin American Studies, its interdisciplinary coursework complementing my political science major. Book learning, however, was not enough. I spent the following quarter at my college's Overseas Center in Santiago, Chile, examining issues of Latin American development in seminars with the field's leading scholars. I also supplemented my academic understanding of Latin America with a more grassroots approach: backpacking extensively through the Andean region. Purposely straying from the tourist-trodden paths, I trekked through the Peruvian jungles and into the Ecuadorian countryside, from capital cities to indigenous villages. I no longer had to conceptualize abstractly a situation in which ninety percent of a nation's wealth is concentrated in the hands of ten percent of its people. I had been directly exposed to the realities of Latin America.

Further investigation of these social inequities included my conducting honors research at the United Nations Economic Commission for Latin America, headquartered in Santiago, Chile. While working at the United Nations, I came to appreciate the importance of mutual respect within the context of multinational interaction; a country's dignity must not be overlooked. Keeping this in mind, I believe we must approach Latin American issues with a better understanding of Latin American perspectives. I hope to use my legal education in conjunction with my interest in Third World development to enhance Latin America's position in the world economic structure. Whether my future includes negotiating international trade agreements, challenging immigration legislation, or providing legal assistance to the Hispanic Community, I look forward to being an advocate for "el pueblo"—the people.

Essays by Multifaceted Applicants

("I'm so well-rounded that my mother calls me 'sun.'")

[While many applicants might mistakenly dismiss their hobbies and extracurricular activities as too irrelevant or insignificant to write about, this applicant draws on these experiences to paint a picture of himself as an adventurous, interesting, and broad-minded individual— just the sort of applicant most schools are looking for.]

My extracurricular life in college was not full of the standard socializing and all-too-common heavy drinking. I spent my free time volunteering as a disk jockey at the college radio station, where I frequently filled in for other DJs' late night time slots, as well as maintaining my own weekly show. I maintained a dormitory-wide collection for the University Recycling Effort and volunteered my arms for the campus-wide collection truck. For recreation I enjoyed playing indoor soccer, biking, canoeing, and spelunking in some very harrowingly tight squeezes that provided claustrophobic character building. Having thoroughly enjoyed acting during my high school years, and having portrayed both the romantic lead of Ferdinand in Shakespeare's The Tempest and a somewhat diabolical Sanson Carasco in Man of La Mancha, I also enjoyed an occasional fantasy role-playing game with friends at college.

During my sophomore year I made friends with a visiting Soviet exchange student and invited him home for the Christmas holidays. By the time he left the United States we were good friends and had taught each other much about our respective cultures. I maintain communication with him to this day and am both proud of and concerned for my friend and his family during the tough times they face. As a junior I spent a semester in Stockholm, Sweden, rediscovering my Swedish ethnic roots, speaking the language and making friends with whom I still correspond. This experience has also enabled me to interact meaningfully with the Swedish clients at the firm for which I work. I am currently taking Spanish courses at night to augment my three years of high school Spanish. With my healthy respect for and experience with other cultures and languages, I welcome the democratic challenges of an increasingly multiethnic and multicultural America.

I have emerged from my schooling and from the world of work with a well-rounded experience in various methods of discourse, scholarly research, composition, real-world stress management and personal responsibility.

[This applicant focused on two particular areas of interest (that are also interesting to read about), then related those interests to his career goals.]

As an undergraduate, I maintained an active involvement with the performing arts. A special interest of mine was improvisational theater, a demanding kind of performance requiring the ability to think on one's feet and, spontaneously, to make a situation convincing and coherent for the audience. "Improv" sharpened my ability to think clearly in a pressured situation—a valuable skill in law school and in a legal career.

I declared a major in sociology and also took several creative writing classes. In both my creative and expository work, I was drawn to taking apart and trying to understand social interaction. This fascination led me to the study of interpersonal communication, specifically conversation analysis. I made detailed transcriptions of taped doctor/patient conversations and analyzed them in terms of the "process of talk." Levels of power and control, efforts to "save face," layers of hidden meaning, and methods of bringing out information are all to be found in everyday conversation, and my studies made me acutely aware of their existence. Attention to detail, a focus on social problems and realistic analyses of causes and solutions were all part of my sociological education.

I entered an M.A./Ph.D. program in sociology in 1992, intending to continue my studies of social interaction. I spent two full semesters and one summer enrolled in this program. Searching for practical applications for my research, I wrote a report on the relevance of social psychology to lawyer-witness interviews. My professor was concerned that this work was "not sociological enough." It was time for a change.

. . . I have not "always wanted to be a lawyer," and I believe this has worked to my advantage. My diverse interests in acting, writing and sociology have contributed to my desire and preparedness for the study of law. I look forward to a legal career in which I can use my past experiences and skills in a creative and practical manner.

[Here is an ingenious and witty response to a question about how the applicant's background and experiences might contribute to the diversity of the school's environment.]

The Renaissance Man: A man who is knowledgeable in an unusually wide variety of the arts and sciences (*World Book Dictionary*). Well, no, I am not yet a Renaissance man. I do try to learn something new every day, and I am always open to new experiences. In order to satisfy my curiosity while in college, I pursued a double major in anthropology and economics. I would go from a class on Game Theory or Industrial Organization to the next class on Foucault or Ethnographic Methodology. I can talk as knowledgeably about the Kula of the Trobriander Islanders as I can about 403(b) and TAMRA guidelines.

In answering this question, I came up with an egocentrically long list detailing my "diversity" and possible contributions to your program. However, here are just six pieces of evidence: 1) I enjoyed *All Quiet on the Western Front* so much that I learned German to read the original version; 2) I play Chopin for stress relief with an emphasis on his nocturnes and preludes; 3) I tried Uni (sea urchin gonad sushi) and liked it; 4) For a class extra-credit project, I co-produced a 16 minute all-in-Japanese video about why young Japanese women come to America; 5) I do computer consulting on the side and am a $50/hour expert in word processing, spreadsheets, and database programming; 6) I am known as [nickname] in the world of bulletin boards and the internet.

I represent your typical well-rounded cultural anthropologist who has experience in financial sales and management. I can contribute computer, ethnographic, and financial expertise.

PART 4

Advice from the Experts

Perhaps the most valuable admissions advice—directly from the decision-makers themselves—is provided right here in Part 4. The admissions officials who are the subjects of the interviews in this part were asked to comment about personal statements, letters of recommendation, personal interviews, and the admissions process generally. Considered together, their comments and advice will provide you with a great deal of insight into the admissions process and what it is the schools really want from their applicants. Of course, if you are applying for admission to any one of the specific schools represented here, you will want to pay particular attention to that interview.

To benefit the greatest number of readers, the schools selected for this part represent a broad cross-section of law, business, and medical schools. The schools included vary greatly in location (all major geographic regions of the country are represented), in size (number of students enrolled), and in type (private and public). And, of course, each admissions official interviewed brings a different perspective to the admissions process.

Advice from the Law Schools

Edward Tom
Director of Admissions
Boalt Hall (University of California at Berkeley,
School of Law)

About the Admissions Process Generally . . .

First we are looking for academic potential in our entering class. But as a close second, we're looking for diversity. Diversity for us goes beyond just racial or ethnic diversity. We're looking for significant representation of older students, people who grew up on the farm as well as those from the city, people from the sciences as well as the liberal arts, a rough parity of men and women, and geographic diversity. The gathering of a diverse range of people like this into a law school classroom really improves the caliber of dialogue that goes on in the law school classroom. A lot of people feel they have to set themselves apart, perhaps by interning at a law office or by going to work for a couple of years after graduation. However, this will not necessarily make a difference because so many people do the same thing. Of course, if you are 10 to 15 years out of school, that's an entirely different set of circumstances.

I am empowered by the faculty to admit half of the entering class. I read roughly 60% of the files from the applicant pool; my assistant reads the other 40%. Of the group that I read, I will administratively admit a sufficient number to enroll half the class, and I will identify other files for further review by the admissions committee. The committee includes faculty and students who are empowered to admit the other half of the class; and they will also create a waiting list—both a resident list and a nonresident list.

About Personal Statements . . .

We ask for one personal statement, and we don't specify a topic; we view this an opportunity to inform us about anything subjective that the applicant might want us to know. The most overused format is the narrative resume, and it doesn't work very well. Applicants can include a resume in their application; but their personal statement should focus on what they want us to know about them that is not readily available from a resume or other parts of their application. We would encourage applicants to write their personal statement in the first person and avoid using styles like poetry or rhyme that are not conducive to our learning about the applicants.

Substantively, the applicant's ambitions are not central to what we are looking for. Our mission is to select law students, not lawyers. Otherwise, the sky is the limit. Some applicants talk about a particular compelling life experience—either positive or negative; some focus on one or two interesting things they have done. For some applicants there are anomalous factors or events that they might want to tell us about—that bout with mononucleosis during the sophomore year that caused their grades to go down one semester or their history of poor standardized testing. I would discourage applicants from using their personal statement to discuss such anomalies. Instead, applicants should prepare an addendum—a separate piece of paper that they attach to their personal statement, entitle that page "My Sophomore Year," for example, and write a few paragraphs to concentrate on that particular anomaly. As for explaining low LSAT scores by discussing a history of poor standardized testing, that is a hard argument for an applicant to make to us because the LSAT is not the same as the SAT or even the GRE. Nevertheless, if we see documented proof—for example, a mediocre LSAT score but a stellar undergraduate record, some consideration will be given to that.

As a related matter, we are seeing applicants with dyslexia in increasing numbers. We encourage them to take the LSAT with accommodations, because they will perform their best that way. We're trying to judge them on their ability, not their disability. We ask them to send copies of all of their application materials to our campus disabled students program where there are experts on dyslexia available if we need them to verify and interpret various diagnostic test scores. Nevertheless, the dyslexic applicant still must be competitive within the general applicant pool. We want to take into account when the disability was diagnosed and when the applicant received accommodations as an undergraduate student, if any at all, because that will affect how we look at the GPA.

About Letters of Recommendation . . .

As a general rule of thumb, a small number—two or at most three—of very good letters is better than a large number that are superficial. The best kinds of letters come from academic sources—professors, T.A.s [teacher assistants]. Sometimes a T.A. will write a much more helpful letter than the professor will, simply because the T.A. has had more one-on-one contact with the individual. The second-best kind of letter comes from an employer who has directly supervised the applicant, especially if the applicant has been employed in a position of responsibility. Letters from famous people, judges, or relatives who are attorneys don't work.

Richard Geiger
Dean of Admissions
Cornell University Law School

About Personal Statements . . .

The biggest mistake applicants make is to bite off more than they can chew by trying to make their personal statement an epic or a life story. One of the keys to success is finding something manageable that still conveys some substance to the reader; that is the challenge. I tell applicants that they should approach the personal statement like an *interview* in which there is a limited amount of time and opportunity to convey something about oneself. Accordingly, applicants should try to think of one or two points or *themes* that they would want to convey to an interviewer about themselves and then make absolutely sure they get those points across.

One statement is all we ask for. We don't have any formal space requirements; length doesn't concern me too much. It's not unheard of for people to submit more than one statement, but it's not that common. When I see more than one essay, I figure the applicant has done it for a reason, and I usually try to figure out the reason. In fact, I encourage applicants to attach a short addendum to their personal statement if they absolutely feel they need to explain deficiencies or weaknesses. My personal view, however, is that it is a mistake to use the personal statement *itself* for that. I prefer to see the personal statement used to convey something positive and affirmative about the applicants, that they would want the reader of the application to know about them, that isn't apparent from the rest of the application.

I think of the personal statement and the LSAT writing sample as fairly distinct. I know of no way to use the LSAT writing sample to corroborate the authenticity of the personal statement. The LSAT writing sample might in some cases, however, allow us to identify weaknesses in writing ability that may not be apparent in a personal statement. The LSAT writing sample is also useful to give us a very broad brush sense of whether the person has the beginnings of the ability to make an argument, to follow the thread of thoughts, and to spot issues.

About Letters of Recommendation . . .

We go into the letters of recommendation to help flesh out the academic record and for some insight into character. We really care a lot about the kind of people who attend our school. Although academics are also very important, law school is not *just* an academic pursuit. I don't want people here who look to be outstanding students if they aren't good people, too. We are relatively small, and the quality of the educational experience depends very much on the quality of the individuals who make up our student body.

We provide a form for recommenders to fill in at their option. We appreciate it when they do fill in the form in addition to writing a separate letter. We ask for two letters of recommendation. For applicants who are current or recent students, we want the letters to be from faculty who have taught them. For applicants who are not recent students, letters from employers or supervisors are fine. In fact, if the applicant has been out of school for several years, I wouldn't be satisfied with old letters of recommendation from a college placement file. I would wonder why the person hadn't come up with *current* recommendations. If someone wants to send academic recommendations that they put on file with their college placement office ten years ago, those satisfy our requirements, and they are free to do so. But in the best interests of filling in the gaps in their application and answering the questions that we are no doubt going to ask, they would probably be better off to give us something more current as well.

About Personal Interviews . . .

We conduct evaluative interviews at our invitation. We may extend an invitation for any number of reasons—for instance, because we want to follow up on something or because we have questions about the applicant that are unanswered by the application. In some years we conduct 200 to 250 interviews—not a very large portion of the applicant pool. We also invite anybody who is on our summer waiting list to have a personal interview at his or her option. Not very many schools do this.

Andy Cornblatt
Assistant Dean of Admissions
Georgetown University Law Center

About Personal Statements . . .

I completely understand the frustration that law-school applicants feel in not having the opportunity to meet us so that we can get to know them in person. But your application is your opportunity to do that, so use it well, and don't be afraid to let me see who you are—particularly through your personal statement. Present yourself in a way that the reader—the admissions officer—can get a good sense of who you really are. Don't try to keep a wall up between us; we call this a *personal* statement, not just a statement. The more open you are, the better we get to know you. I recommend a test to determine whether you're on the right track with your personal statement. When you are done, show it to a friend or family member and ask: "If you never met me before, would you know me better now having read the statement?" If the answer is yes, then you are on the right track. If the answer is no, then you had better go back and do it again.

Give us a sense for who you *really* are. Consider emphasizing an activity you are involved in, how you grew up, or a particular work or travel experience. You can even discuss political issues. Don't be concerned about offending the reader with your views; it really makes no difference whether your views come from the left or the right. Our student body is very diverse—politically and in every other way, and our admissions process is not about political correctness. Finally, if you want to tell us why you want to go to law school or what you are going to do with your law degree, that's fine, but you should not feel obligated to do so.

Some applicants feel frustrated by the application process because they wish to explain some aspect of their application or some event in their life, but the application doesn't allow for it. Perhaps you were ill during a particular semester, or something happened in your life that would explain some aspect of your record, or there is some other information that you feel you want us to know that we don't already know. Feel free to use an *addendum* for that purpose; we will gladly accept it. Unless it fits easily into the theme of your personal statement, I would not suggest that you make it part of your personal statement.

If you would like to send supporting materials—theses, newspaper articles, videotapes, and so forth—that's fine. I want to know who you are when I'm done reviewing your file, and if certain supplementary information helps to give me a three-dimensional view of you, then submit it. Keep in mind however, that it is unlikely that we will read a thesis or other lengthy submission. Also, don't try to be too cute or clever about what you submit. Although I encourage applicants to be creative, don't make us feel as if you submitted something just to show us how clever you are. In other words, don't submit "window dressing" just to show off.

About Letters of Recommendation . . .

Letters of recommendation give us a sense of what the recommender thinks about you in evaluative terms. However, they are also helpful for *informational* purposes. For instance, while you—the applicant—can proclaim yourself to be very involved in all sorts of activities by listing them in your application, it is far more persuasive when that information comes from another source such as a faculty member, dean, or coach. This is also true if you have had a very demanding curriculum or if you have mixed "indicators"—for example, a high GPA and low LSAT score, or the reverse. If there's a reason for it, or if a faculty member can comment on it, that's very, very valuable. If those explanations and elaborations can come from somebody besides you—if your recommender can say, for instance, "I know that her LSAT score is low, but I've had her in class, and take my word for it, the LSAT doesn't matter in this case; she's terrific"—that carries a lot more weight than *your* telling us: "Disregard my LSAT score; I'm a better student than that."

We require two letters of recommendation—a Dean's Certification and one other letter. Perhaps 30 to 40 percent of the dean's forms that we receive are from deans who actually know the applicant and can talk about the applicant as a person. In these cases, the Certification really does become a letter of recommendation. Don't worry, however, if you do not know your dean personally. The main purpose of the Certification is to confirm certain information in your file. The additional letter of recommendation should be from a professor, although if you have been out of undergraduate school for five years or more, we understand that it may be more difficult for you to get a letter from a professor. If any applicant wishes to submit more than one additional letter, that is just fine, although I suggest that applicants submit no more than three (in addition to the Dean's Certification). If you wish us to hear from two professors and an employer, for example, I have no problem with that. Faculty recommenders do not have to be faculty in your major. I want to hear from the professors who know you best. Also, a letter from a full professor with some degree of notoriety or status but who doesn't know you very well is not nearly as helpful to me as a letter from someone who knows you better. Finally, give the recommender a little guidance that will help him or her in writing a letter for you. Faculty members will appreciate and not resent guidance on your part.

Many applicants are concerned about whether they should waive their right of access to the letters of recommendation. First of all, it's not a major decision, and if it doesn't matter all that much to you, then waive access. Most faculty members will let you see what they wrote if you ask them, anyway, so it's usually not a big issue. For 80 to 90 percent of the recommendation letters that we receive, the applicants have waived access. You will not be penalized in any way for *not* waiving access. However, by your not waiving access, it could be construed that the letter of recommendation may not be as open and honest as it otherwise might have been.

About the Admissions Process Generally . . .

Like most law schools, we have a rolling admissions system, which simply means that we consider applications as soon as they are complete and in the order in which they are completed. Therefore, the sooner you apply, the better your chances of admission. I recommend that applicants take the LSAT no later than October of the year before they plan to matriculate and get their applications in by Thanksgiving so that we can begin the decision-making process in December. However, if December is a better time for you to take the test, that is just fine and you will not be disadvantaged. We let applicants know about our decision right away.

Dennis Shields
Assistant Dean and Director of Admissions
The University of Michigan Law School

About Personal Statements . . .

We give the opportunity to write three essays—one is a required personal statement while the other two essays are optional. Don't use your required personal statement to recap your resume. Use it to highlight a few things that will really give us some insight into you as a person—you might, for example, discuss a significant activity of yours that is indicative of the kind of person you are. We don't impose a length restriction on our required personal statement; such a restriction would take some of the judgment that we're looking for away from the candidates. Bear in mind, however, that the reader probably has 10 to 20 minutes to read and respond to your essays and letters of recommendation. So say everything you think is important in a length that is manageable to get through within this time frame.

In our first optional essay, applicants are asked to focus on aspects of their background and experiences which will contribute to the diversity our law school wishes to foster. Whether an applicant should respond to this question is a real judgment call for the applicant. Everyone is different in some way, but you have to ask yourself whether there's a clear distinction in your life experience that would warrant your taking a couple of pages to tell someone how you're different. The critical thing about this essay is not just saying how you are different but showing some ability to talk about it in a way that makes clear how this difference would benefit the educational endeavor of this institution. When I see a laundry list of everything the applicant has participated in, my response is: you and everybody else. What about those experiences will be of significance when you're sitting in contracts class during the first year of law school? Why would a faculty member or your classmates care about your experiences? How have they given you special insights?

The second optional essay calls for applicants to let us know about the way they think. People make a real error when they don't write that essay. The ability to write an essay about something other than yourself and to show some real insight and thought gives us a sense of the quality of your writing, your intellect and your education. This essay is very important; in fact, for some people, it's critical. When I am looking at two candidates in the middle of the applicant pool who are equally qualified, and I can only admit one of them, I am going to admit the one who writes a good essay that shows introspection, circumspection, some real ability to see both sides of an issue and to talk about them. I don't care if anyone says anything about law in this essay or shows any real insight into the law; and I don't like a lot of legal jargon. I want applicants to write about something they really care about, but something that they can still separate themselves from to look at fairly analytically and critically and to communicate that in a coherent fashion.

Make your essays readable and manageable in length. Avoid using tiny fonts, small margins or small spacing. Don't think that your file is going to be read at 10 o'clock in the morning after the reader's first cup of coffee; assume instead that it's 2 o'clock in the morning and yours is the last of many files the reader is going to look at for the day. If you were the reader, how would you like something to look under these circumstances, and how long would you want it to be if you were going to read it carefully in 10 to 20 minutes? Finally, don't send us your Ph.D. thesis, a bunch of newspaper clippings . . . that sort of thing; we're not going to look at them.

About Letters of Recommendation . . .

We require at least one letter of recommendation. People routinely send us more than one, and we don't hold that against them. Remember, though, that the reader has only 15 to 30 minutes to read your file, and you don't want too much in your file for the reader to get through in this limited time. We don't need character references. What we want is an academic reference in every case where it's possible. The academic record is all important because law school is an academic pursuit. We want to get impressions of the applicant from somebody who has had this person in class and has seen his or her work product. We realize that it's hard for people who have attended public institutions to find a faculty member who knows them well enough to write something for them that would be useful; but they really do need an academic reference. If you have been out of school for a while and have lost touch with your college instructors, letters from a placement file at the college are acceptable even though they're not current.

About Personal Interviews . . .

We don't conduct evaluative interviews. However, we make every effort to talk to any applicant who wants to talk to us. We'll look at the applicant's file and indicate whether there is something we have a question about or whether there's a way to improve the file . . . that sort of thing. I wouldn't characterize that as an interview, however.

Shelli Soto
Director of Admissions
The University of Texas at Austin, School of Law

About the Admission Process Generally . . .

Considering the 4,000-plus applications that we receive every year, if we were to rely strictly on the undergraduate grades and LSAT scores in making admissions decisions, our median numbers would be far above what they actually are. The range of GPAs and LSAT scores from applicants to the top law schools really is evidence that personal statements, resumes, and recommendation letters make a huge difference. We rely on this information to bring diversity to the class. We want interesting people whose differing life experiences will bring a different perspective to the discussion and study of law and who will contribute to the profession, not just people who have managed to study successfully.

Like many of our peer schools, we have moved away from a committee review process to an administrative one. With committee review, each reader would review only a small portion of the applicant pool. Under our administrative system, files are reviewed by a faculty member and two admissions professionals, one of whom reads every file to become familiar with the entire applicant pool. With fewer people in touch with a broader section of the applicant pool, we can make more informed judgments.

About Personal Statements . . .

The topic for the personal statement is a matter of personal choice. Because we require a resume with our application, applicants should not use the personal statement to provide a narrative of their work experience, extracurricular activities, or other chronological listing of accomplishments. I prefer personal statements that focus on something unique to the applicant. I advise applicants to focus on some past experience, perhaps something about their family or about a particular accomplishment, that is really striking—something that is going to stand out to the reader. It just makes sense to me that if somebody remembers reading your personal statement, this will increase your chance of admission. However, you don't want to get too outrageous. A personal statement can also be memorable because it made a negative impression.

I read a wonderful personal statement this year—one that really stood out for me—about the applicant's experiences volunteering at an AIDS shelter. It was not a global explanation of all of his volunteer service but rather a very concise, tightly written essay that just told about his experience with one of the people in the AIDS shelter. That essay really caught my attention and stood out in my mind. Statements like that really do make a difference. He commented about how that whole experience made him a better person. That's always a good angle to take with a personal statement. It's always a good idea to focus on how the experience has affected you rather than just telling the story.

We see many personal statements in which the applicants talk about why they want to be a lawyer. The applicant might say: "I've wanted to be a lawyer since I was ten" or "Grandpa was a lawyer" or "I think it's a noble profession." We are more interested in gaining some insight into who the applicant is at this point in his or her life rather than about his or her goals and ambitions. Of course some applicants have very definite ideas about what they want to do . . . perhaps they want to work in public interest law or in the area of international trade, and a legal education is part of the preparation for the specific goal. Those kinds of personal statements can be very effective, but only if the ambition seems to be something very consistent and compelling based upon our review of the entire file and our overall picture of the person.

We place a two-page limit on the personal statement. Our application also requests information about prior matriculation in law school, prior criminal record, or disciplinary actions by an institution of higher learning. Those questions, if answered affirmatively, require a separate statement. Applicants should know that these statements are not part of the personal statement and do not count against the page limitation of the personal statement.

About Letters of Recommendation . . .

We do not require letters of recommendation, although they are strongly encouraged. Most of our applicants submit recommendation letters to us, and we encourage it. I feel that those applicants who do not submit recommendation letters are at somewhat of a disadvantage because so many applicants do submit them and because they can be quite helpful. Letters from faculty members who have worked closely with the applicant are generally most helpful. Students from small schools typically have no problem getting faculty letters. On the other hand, students applying from very large universities have limited opportunities to get well acquainted with their professors. Those students may be better off obtaining a letter from an employer, co-worker, or perhaps a teaching assistant—somebody who knows them well, rather than a faculty member who can only say that the applicant "got an A in my class." Letters from a credential or recommendation service or placement file at the applicant's undergraduate institution are perfectly acceptable. Otherwise, we encourage applicants to send the letters in sealed envelopes along with the application.

About the LSAT Writing Sample . . .

All too often, people don't take the LSAT writing sample seriously enough. The LSAT writing sample is important and really is helpful to us because it indicates whether the person possesses the fundamental writing skills that are needed for legal research and writing. If a writing sample suggests to me that this person has poor writing skills, that might be a factor in the admissions decision.

Michael Rappaport
Dean of Admissions
UCLA School of Law

About Personal Statements . . .

We want to know what is different or unusual about you—what you can contribute or bring to the first-year classroom that would be unique. Perhaps you've held a job for five years and you have some real world experience; perhaps you speak several languages; perhaps you've overcome some disadvantage; or perhaps you are merely applying from out of state. These are the kinds of things you might want to talk about since they would distinguish you from other applicants. We are not particularly interested in why you want to go to law school or what you want to do when you get out, since these things change. And don't tell us that you want to be a Supreme Court justice or United States senator; anyone can say that.

Admittedly, most applicants—particularly those coming right out of college—have a great deal of difficulty distinguishing themselves from others. We recognize that problem. The typical successful admitted student is about 21 years old, is bright, has engaged in various extra-curricular activities during college, perhaps has done some volunteer work, and so forth. For such people, we have to fall back on their academic records. If they have the grades and test scores, the presumption is that they will get in. We are not going to deny someone because the applicant can't distinguish himself or herself from everyone else. So to these applicants I would say: don't worry too much about your personal statement; just don't say something really stupid.

It's fine to take some risks and submit something unusual, but it depends upon what it is. Once in a while we see something that catches our eye—for example, a photograph that accompanies the applicant's story about what he or she did in the Peace Corps. I wouldn't request something like that, but it is an attention getter. Humor is fine; it's a welcome break, as long as it is actually humorous. I hate seeing essays that begin with something like: "In the matter before the court of UCLA, regarding the admission of. . . ." Everyone who uses this approach thinks it is unique, but it's not. We don't want a copy of your 150-page thesis; we are not going to read it. Instead, you might talk about the thesis or submit a letter of recommendation from someone who has read the thesis who could tell us about it.

Look at the personal statement as perhaps one of the most important briefs you'll ever write. This essay is going to be read for the most part by law professors who are going to take a red pencil to every misspelled word and grammatical error. When an applicant fails to proofread adequately, I wonder what kind of attorney that applicant could make.

About Letters of Recommendation . . .

A letter of recommendation that says, for example: "This is the best student I've had in 25 years of teaching" will obviously make a difference; and if you say something in your application which appears outlandish, a letter of recommendation to back up what you are saying in your application is important. Otherwise, 99 percent of the letters of recommendation that we get are all essentially the same: "[The applicant] was a student in my class; she's bright, she's motivated. . . ." It's fine to have a letter like that in your file; if this sort of letter *wasn't* there, our eyebrows might be raised. But this kind of letter is not going to be the controlling factor in our admission decision because nearly every other applicant is going to have essentially the same letter.

Advice from the Business Schools

Ethan Hanabury
Associate Dean for Admissions and Administration
Columbia University, Graduate School of Business

About the Admissions Process Generally . . .

A much more subjective or qualitative assessment is involved in the admissions process than one might assume. Undergraduate grades and GMAT scores enter into our assessment, but they are not the driving force in our decision making. Because we are trying to determine who will be the strongest and the best business leaders, we must also assess interpersonal skills, work experience, and personal attributes. Because of this, it is very important how one presents oneself in the application. We are also continuing to increase the number of evaluative interviews that we offer; these help us to assess whether the applicant will be successful at Columbia and successful in business.

About Personal Statements . . .

In the essays, we are particularly interested in what applicants plan to do after business school and how that relates to what they have done in the past. We look closely at their past work experiences. Typically, our students come to us with at least 3 or 4 years of work experience. We look at that experience and what they have accomplished whether, for example, they have been able to lead other people or have at least demonstrated some leadership potential. How well the applicant works with other people as a member of a team is very important to us because in business school students work in group projects and because in the corporate world the ability to get along with and work with others is crucial to success.

We are also interested in the applicant's level of interest in and knowledge about Columbia. We are looking for a fit—for the type of person who will succeed in this particular environment. Columbia is located in New York City, and much of the curriculum and activities take advantage of this location. It takes a certain type of person—someone who appreciates the stimulation and diversity that surrounds us—to succeed here. Our student body is very cosmopolitan and international. About 25-30% of our students come from countries other than the U.S. Our domestic applicants tend to be very international as well, in that some of them were born outside the U.S. and many of them have traveled and worked abroad. An applicant who has stayed in one type of environment and hasn't really looked at different ways of doing things—by traveling, doing a term abroad, or working with underprivileged kids, for instance—is probably not well suited for Columbia. This doesn't mean that we don't take into account that some people have had more opportunities in their early lives than others. If we can sense through the application that an applicant has taken advantage of every opportunity that *has* been available to learn about other cultures and other ways of doing things, then we recognize that this is the type of person who would take advantage of the opportunity to attend our school.

Gimmicks and attention-grabbing statements are unnecessary and are effective in an essay only if the applicant can tie them in with something about themselves that is distinctive. We received samples of fruit juice once from an applicant who started a fruit juice company, and that made a good impression; we could see the proof that this person really did start this business, and that was a nice touch; but it certainly wasn't necessary. What's most important is that applicants assess themselves and that who they are gets through in the application. We're not looking for every single person to be a genius and be perfect in all regards; most people have some blemish in their past. We're looking for people who are real, who have good plans for the future, and who have the capacity to succeed.

We expect that many applicants, particularly international students, have had help in writing their essays, and it's perfectly all right for an applicant to get help with the mechanics. However, when we see a perfectly-written essay from an international student, we wonder who really wrote the essay.

About Letters of Recommendation . . .

We require two letters of recommendation, and we prefer that they be from employers or supervisors, not from faculty; we rely on the GMAT and undergraduate transcripts for evaluating applicants academically. Sometimes we sense that the recommender has allowed the applicant to write the letter, especially if it's too gimmicky or if it sounds like a sales pitch. We really are looking to get the most information we can about the applicant from the recommender, and the only way to help us is for the recommender to actually write it.

Melinda Bissett
Director of Admissions
The Fuqua School of Business (Duke University)

About the Admissions Process Generally . . .

We review personal statements and letters of recommendation from every single applicant. There is no GMAT score that guarantees admission and no score that guarantees that an applicant will be denied. Certainly, someone well below average in multiple categories has a tough road simply because it's a competitive process. However, we go through the same process in terms of reading the file, making notes, and bringing the file up at committee, for every application. We have six readers—three professional staff and three readers—whom we hire for the reading season to review about 2,500 applications. In order to relate to the process, the readers that we hire have had either admissions experience or business experience similar to what our applicants have had.

About Personal Statements . . .

Showing that you have spent time thinking about why an MBA is important to you and how it can be useful to you is a critical part of the essay. I've seen essays that say essentially: "I want to be CEO of a small, medium, or large-size firm." That's weak. Put some serious thought into it. Having no career direction is not impressive. By the same token, applicants don't have to be highly specific in their career goals. Certainly some people have had more exposure to business, and we would expect a sharper focus from them. Most applicants don't have a clear direction; many are coming to business school to clarify their direction a bit more; we don't hold this against them. Others—for example, those who have been in the military—may be less focused simply because civilian life is quite different from military life; yet they still must show that they have given serious thought as to why an MBA is important to them. If you haven't gone through that thought process and can't articulate it on an application, I'm not sure you are doing the best thing by applying to an MBA program.

Try to make a reasonably objective assessment of your strengths and weaknesses. If your weaknesses are rather clear, admit them and show how you have learned from them. Acknowledge your 2.4 GPA, for example, and talk about it. If you are pretty honest, that comes through, we appreciate it, and your interests are better served. Also, say something rather concrete about why the particular school is a good place for you. Take the time to make the essay different for the different schools that you are applying to. Many applicants submit the same essay to multiple schools and forget to change the name of the school for each application. It's not fatal, but this does give us insight into their thoroughness and how much time they spent on their application.

About Letters of Recommendation . . .

We require three letters of recommendation, and recommendations certainly can make a difference. We would much rather have current recommendations. Some applicants think they have to find a professor for a recommendation. However, recommendations from professors are usually not that helpful. When applicants have been out of school for a few years or more, their professors don't know how they have grown and matured since their undergraduate years and therefore can't relate to the questions we are asking. Letters of recommendation from applicants' placement files at their undergraduate institution are pretty useless for the same reason.

I would encourage applicants to think about their choice of recommenders carefully and pursue every avenue to come up with at least two that are work related. It would be nice to have all three be professionally related. Otherwise, I would rather see a current recommendation from someone, for example, with a community organization that the applicant is involved with now than something that is old. We realize that people can't always tell everybody at their workplace about their plans to go to business school since doing so may hurt them career-wise. However, there may be one person at work whom the applicant can trust enough to ask for a letter of recommendation. Perhaps a past supervisor or coworker who is no longer with the organization could provide a recommendation . . .

We see some name dropping; but most MBA applicants are savvy enough to realize that it is not in fact always "who you know." People in power positions don't affect what goes on at the school enough to make a difference. If that person cannot say anything of use to the admissions committee, then to us the recommendation is insignificant. A recommendation from the President of the United States is not exciting if the President does not know the applicant personally and cannot talk about his or her leadership, interpersonal, and teamwork skills. What is the President going to do to us if we don't admit this person? Not much!

Paul Magelli
Assistant Dean
University of Illinois M.B.A. Program

About the Admissions Process Generally . . .

Because of new leadership here in the College of Business, we are a bit of a johnny-come-lately in the competition which has heated up during the last 12 to 15 years among M.B.A. programs. One of the initiatives required to catch up relates to the quality of students the school can attract. What business schools look for ultimately is *placeability*—how that student is likely to fare out of business school in competition for a job in a tightening marketplace. Thus, a strong admissions program is dependent upon a strong placement program, especially at private schools, where students are making a significant monetary investment and want to know what the payoff is going to be.

How do we determine *placeability*? Although we look at the applicant's quantitative skills as determined by the GMAT quantitative score and the undergraduate record, I refuse to be GMAT-driven or quantitatively-driven. Instead, what I am looking for primarily (and what I think my colleagues at other schools are looking for, regardless of what they might print) is a candidate that has a certain *persona*—a cluster of characteristics that includes wisdom, maturity, articulateness, intuitiveness, assertiveness, caringness, analytical skills, and presentation skills. This cluster or package correlates more highly with success in an M.B.A. program here or anywhere else than any other characteristic, period.

About Personal Statements and Letters of Recommendation . . .

I can recognize that *persona [see above]* in a candidate, quite honestly, in about five minutes if he or she is standing in front of me. If not, I can ascertain this with a bit less certainty by talking to the candidate's colleagues—perhaps those who wrote letters of recommendation—or by talking to the candidate by telephone. The recommendation letters themselves are not very helpful, nor are the candidate's essays. Although we read them and take them seriously, the essays are staid, conservative, and cautiously written—for the most part very "establishment." So you have a nice articulate essay. Who wrote the essay? I'm looking for that *persona*.

About Personal Interviews . . .

If you have this cluster of what we are looking for *[see above]*, then it will emerge during an interview. We certainly honor every student's request for an evaluative interview, and requests for interviews are increasing. We're now moving into evaluative interviews on *our* option because we want to see if we can ascertain this thing I call *persona*. If we are going to deny admission, we want to have a very strong and valid reason. The interview is more important and credible than any other single criterion. This is especially true for candidates with low quantitative scores on the GMAT; an interview affords them an opportunity to sell themselves.

Many candidates who come to us for interviews have also interviewed elsewhere and have been disappointed with the quality of the interviews at some of the more prestigious schools. For example, the candidate may have talked with one or two students during the interview process but not with any member of the professional staff. Candidates cannot help but wonder why this is the case, especially when the school requires an interview. If candidates make the effort to visit us in person, we want to make sure that at least four or five of us see them and give them the opportunity to make their case. I wouldn't say we provide the ultimate campus visit, but when students come here for a visit, they meet the admissions staff, the program directors, students, perhaps one or more faculty members, as well as visiting several classes. An individual program is made up for them with their name on it. We pay for their overnight visits, and we fly in ethnic minority students at our expense.

Mary Miller
Director of Admissions
Leonard N. Stern School of Business at New York University

About Personal Statements . . .

We want to know about applicants' unique characteristics and what they value in themselves and in others. In order to give applicants the opportunity to share what they think is important about themselves, we keep our questions very open-ended. Nevertheless, you'd be surprised how many applicants write the same things, the canned response, as if we were looking for the "right" answer. Of course there really is no right answer. What we *are* looking for are those applicants who have put some thought into their essays and who accurately convey their personality, their goals, and motivation clearly and concisely. At the same time, applicants should not try to stand out by giving us something gimmicky.

Read the questions carefully and follow the directions. This may seem rather trivial and obvious, but it's not. Part of what we're looking for is to see if the applicant can follow directions. For instance, when we say we want a 200-word essay, we don't mean 2,000 words; the admissions committee looks with some dismay upon essays that go on and on. Also, read the question accurately and respond appropriately. For example, let's look at one of our current essay questions, which involves nominating as a keynote speaker any person living in this century. We get lots of responses nominating people from way, way back in history. This shows a lack of attention to detail.

About Letters of Recommendation . . .

I'm surprised that recommenders are as honest as they are. I find letters of recommendation to be in general very valuable. When you read as many letters as we do, it's obvious whether the recommender knows the individual or just has a cursory interest or a nice title. When recommenders really know the person, they generally give us some very good information, especially about the person's strengths and weaknesses.

About Personal Interviews . . .

We have made a dramatic move toward conducting more interviews. Interviews are still optional, however, and by our invitation only. We invite applicants to interview with us based on an initial review of the application. We read an applicant's entire file prior to the interview. Since we have already read the essays to learn about the applicant's background, personality, and so forth, we can use the interview to key on something in the application that piques our interest and go from there. We don't have to waste time rehashing what the applicant has already stated in the application. Many applicants tell us that they find this approach refreshing because at some other schools the interviewers have not read the essays or even seen the application prior to the interview, so all the applicants do is rehash what they wrote in their application.

Eric C. Abrams
Assistant Director of M.B.A. Admissions
Stanford University, Graduate School of Business

About Personal Statements . . .

Tell us your story using interesting and lively essays. Please understand that *people*, not machines, read the essays. If you had to sift through 15-20 sets of essays every day for six months, what would you want to read? Interesting, lively, occasionally witty stories, right? Us too. Don't try too hard to appear unique, because you can't know what the other people in the applicant pool are like. You don't need to do *anything* you can to stand out, for example, don't submit an essay in crayon, and don't send us a videotape of you and your buddies doing a rap song about why you want to get in. If you are applying to a graduate program in the creative arts, unconventional format might not be a bad idea, but not for law or business.

For whatever reason, applicants frequently try to combine our essay questions with essay questions from other schools that they are applying to, and I can tell immediately upon reading the first couple of paragraphs that they are not really answering our questions. It is important to answer the specific questions of the school you are applying to. A related and common mistake is not fully addressing why you want to go to that particular school. Keep in mind that the people who read these applications often attended the institution or have worked there for a number of years and have an emotional attachment to the school, and so they really want to know your reasons for selecting their particular school. Many applicants give us generic reasons—for example, "I want to go to your institution because you have a strong faculty in finance and marketing, and I think it is one of the best schools in the country." Well, you can say that about a lot of schools. If you are applying to our school just because it is ranked highly by the Gourman Report don't let us figure that out from your application. That's like saying that you are going to root for a particular college basketball team because the preseason polls say that it is going to be number one.

Be sure to explain deficiencies or weaknesses in your application. Perhaps your GPA took a nose-dive for a semester because your parents got divorced during that semester or because your financial aid didn't come through and you had to work forty hours per week just to make ends meet. Explain that to us. What we don't want you to do, however, is whine. Whining as far as I'm concerned is really the kiss of death. Life is hard, and there is a difference between providing an explanation and whining about circumstances. It annoys me when an applicant says, for example: "as vice president of my fraternity I was required to do all this stuff and it cut into my study time," or "during my sophomore year the person I fell in love with my freshman year broke my heart, and that is why I did poorly in school that year." Those sorts of things happen to everybody, and, in truth, those sorts of things are going to arise while in business school.

Some applicants incorporate charts or graphs into their personal statements, but I don't find this very helpful. Narrative explanations are better than graph/chart type explanations, if for no other reason, because the type of people in admissions tend to like to read. You can more fully tell a story about what happened in narrative than by just showing a graph.

Only our admissions staff read the essays. One person will read a file and make a number of comments on it; then someone else gets the file, reads it, and either agrees or disagrees with other comments. The closer you get to being admitted, the more people read your file. Most of the communication among our readers is either on paper or through e-mail.

About Letters of Recommendation . . .

We see name dropping all the time. Some applicants try to find the most famous name or an influential Stanford alumnus to write a letter of recommendation. In truth, that's not what we're looking for. We are looking for people who know you well and have worked closely with you; if they have not, it hurts you. Recommenders who don't know applicants will typically state in their letters that they don't know the applicant well and don't know why the applicant asked them for a letter of recommendation. This gives us a reason to question the applicant's judgment.

Henry F. Malin
Director of Admissions
Amos Tuck School of Business Administration
(Dartmouth College)

About the Admissions Process Generally . . .

There's obviously an objective part to this process in that there are hurdles that are "cleared" using the objective measures. There's also a very subjective part, and in many cases it's the subjective part that drives our decision. Applicants should keep in mind that this process is quite different from applying to college in that you can apply more than once. Many of the people who reapply here get in because there are areas of their application that they have improved. If somebody has a deficiency in the quantitative area, for instance, and addresses it by taking coursework, etc., we may then be able to admit that applicant. It's not a one shot deal. In most cases, the applicant is working and has the option to continue working while he or she reapplies. Of course applicants should find out if reapplying is a real option. Call and ask if it's a matter of working another year—that sort of thing. Like most schools, we try to give meaningful feedback to applicants who haven't been accepted.

About Personal Statements . . .

Good essays will carry an applicant a long way. The essays are the first thing in every applicant's file, aside from a cover sheet that provides some basic information. So the applicants have an opportunity right away to put their best foot forward and give us a great first impression *before* we read what someone else—perhaps a recommender or an interviewer—thinks about them. Applicants should keep in mind that our admissions committee includes several people, most of whom obviously have not met the applicant; so applicants should put enough time into their essays to convey their personality and say what they really want to say, and in a strong way, rather than only counting on the person who interviewed them to go to bat for them.

One of our essay questions asks essentially where you have been, where you are going, and how an M.B.A. fits into all of this. Many applicants tend to think that they must present to us a very clear plan and convince us that every decision they have ever made has been perfectly consistent with this plan. Certainly, we love for people to have some idea about why they're going to spend $80,000 for this degree! But when applicants are too specific about their goals or plans, we begin to write words like "narrow!" in their file. Of course we look for *some* consistency. When applicants say that they want to be investment bankers, for instance, but there is nothing in their background that indicates this and no personal traits that would indicate that investment banking would be a good match, we begin to question their thought processes.

We also ask about the applicant's interests outside of work or school. A lot of applicants treat this as a throwaway essay.

However, for those who choose to make it an integral part of their presentation, it can be very effective and can be a real opportunity. Applicants have discussed such subjects as family, relationship with a spouse, one of their children, or some key event in their life. These kinds of essays can be very effective.

There tends to be a lot of sameness among the business schools in terms of what questions they ask in their applications. We always try to include at least one question that you can't answer by plugging in your response to a question from another school's application. For example, a number of schools ask the applicant to discuss an ethical dilemma they have faced. We don't ask that question, and when we see a discussion about facing an ethical dilemma, it's an immediate tip-off that the applicant has applied to one of these other schools as well.

My general advice: Don't try to fabricate a personality or a life story; we want to admit who you are, not a fictional account of who you are. The people who let us see inside them are the ones we are most attracted to.

About Personal Interviews . . .

Evaluative interviews are highly recommended, and we try to give applicants every opportunity to interview. We interviewed 2,000 people this year out of an applicant pool of 2,200. Because our location is somewhat removed from a major urban area, we travel extensively to 18 domestic cites and five international cities every year. We set up 30-minute appointments, and applicants are not screened for these interviews. We also interview on campus, of course, and we conduct alumni interviews as well.

I can't quantify how important the interview is. For some people, it just confirms everything else that's in the file. Interviews are always conducted *before* we review applications so applicants can start with a clean slate. There is a downside to knowing too much about an applicant before an interview. For example, if you already know the applicant has a really low GMAT score or GPA, your attitude immediately is that this person is going to have to be *really* good to get through this screen. My experience is that if people have a blemish either on their academic record or in their test scores, they will tell us during the interview anyway.

Advice from the Medical Schools

Judy Colwell
Assistant Director of Admissions
Stanford University School of Medicine

About Personal Statements . . .

In most cases the Personal Comment portion of the AMCAS application does not make or break an application, unless the applicant seems to be arrogant or incredibly naive in discussing medicine. Many people discuss who they are in many ways without talking about medicine at all. An outline of accomplishment or a grandiose essay about what a doctor should be doesn't tell as much about who the applicant is and makes it difficult to evaluate him or her. What we want instead in terms of content is for people to tell us who they are. I would encourage them to be themselves and have faith in themselves when writing their personal statements well (as during the interview process). Some personal statements are so wonderfully written that we'll get goose bumps or be in tears. Most applicants don't write so beautifully, of course.

Applicants who call us for advice about writing the AMCAS personal statement are referred to their premed advisors. After reviewing AMCAS applications, we send out supplemental applications to all of those under consideration. Although our supplemental application does not call for a personal statement per se, it does inquire about the applicant's clinical and research activities as well as community service. Community service is very important in our process because this is a profession devoted to serving others. We have one of the longer applications among the medical schools. Applicants either love it or hate it; most love it because we give them a chance to tell us what they want us to know about them.

About Personal Interviews . . .

The number of interviews that we conduct—about 600 each year—is small compared to many other schools because our class size is relatively small. No one is admitted here without interviewing. We do not use field representatives nor alumni for interviewing. Each applicant under consideration comes to campus and is interviewed for approximately an hour by a current medical student and for about an hour by a current faculty member. These are separate interviews, not panel interviews. Interviewees will also tour the medical center and have lunch with the other interviewees of the day with medical students.

Raymond Brienza
Assistant Dean of Admissions
New York University School of Medicine

About the Admissions Process Generally . . .

We do not participate in AMCAS. We have always prided ourselves on paying personal attention to every application. Each application undergoes several reviews by members of our faculty committee. If we were to become an AMCAS school, then the number of applications submitted to us would easily double, and we would no longer be able to read the applications individually. We feel we can find the applicants who would be fine candidates for NYU from an applicant pool of 4,000-4,200 without having to double that number.

About Personal Statements . . .

I tell candidates to make sure they tell us things that are of special interest about themselves in order to add a dimension to the application for the reader. Most importantly, they should explain characteristics and aspects of their background that make them unique. A common mistake that many applicants make is to assume that they will discuss what makes them special or unique at the interview rather than putting it in writing first. However, if they don't put it in writing first so the reader can know, they might not advance to the interview.

Applicants might also consider using the personal statement to explain significant weaknesses and deficiencies. Also, individuals applying for more than the second time must submit a separate written statement explaining their reasons for reapplying and outlining any significant changes since the last application.

About Letters of Recommendation . . .

We require that each applicant have a recommendation submitted by the premedical advisory committee of his or her college. If the college has no committee, applicants should arrange to have letters written by two faculty members, one of which must be from a science teacher, and sent directly to us. Letters from teachers for whom they have done research or in whose lab they have been employed cannot be used to meet this requirement. Only letters from faculty who have taught them in a regular class can be counted. Letters from research mentors can, of course, be sent as additional references. For those individuals who are reapplying, we want to know if any recommendations that were not in the previous application are to be sent; if so, we will wait for these. If we are not so informed, we will process the application on the basis of the previous year's information.

About Personal Interviews . . .

We only have 160 places in our class; from about 4,200 applicants we will interview perhaps just over 900 applicants. To prepare for the interview, candidates ought to talk to someone they have a lot of confidence in—perhaps their premedical advisor—and practice answering questions and work on how they present themselves. We generally conduct just one interview for each applicant. Interviews are about 45 minutes to an hour in length and are with a single interviewer—a member of our faculty who is an experienced member of the admissions committee. The interviewer is given the applicant's folder beforehand and is asked to review it so he or she knows something about the candidate before the interview starts. The applicant will also have lunch with students and take a tour, so it's a three- or four-hour day.

The M.D./Ph.D. coordinators conduct day-long interviews because students have to talk to research scientists as well as to an admissions interviewer; so there will be perhaps four interviews altogether as well as a meeting with current students in the program. Our joint program was the first of its kind sponsored by the National Institute of Health; it is very select and very prestigious.

Katie Horne
Director of Admissions
University of Michigan Medical School

About Personal Statements . . .

We don't screen AMCAS personal statements systematically for certain content. We read the personal statement to assess the person's ability to communicate in writing and for any explanatory information that helps elucidate the academic record and give us a general impression of the person's background and interest in medicine. I tell applicants that this is their chance to tell us about themselves as persons since the rest of the application really doesn't. Tell us not only why you want to be a doctor but what you have done to test your decision. Have you had some experience? Have you observed doctors? Applicants do not by and large discuss the financial motivation for becoming a doctor, and that's probably wise. Occasionally, however, we will see a mention of the stability of the profession as a lifelong career or the rewards in terms of terms of adequacy of support.

One reason why we feel the AMCAS personal statement is so important is that we do not include additional essays on our supplemental form. The supplemental form is strictly a listing of the courses taken to meet our requirements and a list of individuals writing recommendation letters. We are very up-front with applicants that they can send us whatever they want. If they want to send us copies of their publications or a curriculum vitae, for example, we'll put it in their file. Some schools prefer not to do things that way, but we tell applicants that they are putting their best foot forward and can send to us whatever they want to let us know more about them as applicants.

About Letters of Recommendation . . .

We ask for a minimum of three letters: one from science faculty, one from non-science faculty, and one other of the student's choosing. Because so many science majors really don't have a non-science faculty member who knows them well enough to write a strong reference, we will be flexible on the non-science faculty recommendation and will generally waive this requirement at the request of the applicant. Also, they can send us more than three letters if they wish, and it is not unusual for applicants to do so.

Although committee letters are generally very helpful, we don't require them since many undergraduate schools don't provide them. Committee letters can be quite useful because there is usually an advisor involved who has worked with the student over a period of time and who knows the student much better than a faculty member who has only seen the student in one or two courses. Also, a committee letter serves as a means of comparing the applicant with others from that school. By giving a student its "stamp of approval," the committee is saying essentially that this student is the very best from the school this year. Their assessment then becomes important to us, especially if it's a good school in terms of what we have experienced about its previous applicants.

About Personal Interviews . . .

We give each applicant two interviews with members of the admissions committee. One of the interviews is with a faculty member, and the other may be with either a faculty member or a student. Interviews are 30 to 40 minutes each. Occasionally, applicants will request a regional interview, and we use members of our alumni body to conduct these interviews; otherwise, all interviewing is conducted at our school.

Some schools take a systematic interviewing approach in which every applicant is asked certain standard questions. Also, some schools conduct only blind interviews while some conduct only informed interviews. We maintain a more flexible approach in which our interviewers may choose whatever method they prefer. Some of the doctors prefer to close the file and just have the applicants talk, while others like to review the applicant's file thoroughly ahead of time. Applicants should try to anticipate the most common questions and think about how they are going to respond. Of course you can't anticipate every question. However, interviewers almost invariably ask why you want to be a doctor, so you had better have a good answer ready for that one.

Most applicants feel that the earlier they interview at the school of their choice the more likely they are to get an early offer, which in turn allows them to make an early commitment and drop some of the other schools from their interviewing schedule. For this reason, we tend to make more early offers to nonresidents than to residents. In any event, for applicants who are already confident about their interviewing skills, there's no reason why they shouldn't interview as early as possible. Nevertheless, we always try to have some openings in the class whenever students are interviewing, even in March. This is not true at all the schools, especially those on a rolling admissions system.

Diana Woo, M.D.
Associate Dean for Student Affairs
The Pritzker School of Medicine (The University of Chicago)

About Personal Statements . . .

Although what the candidate writes about in the AMCAS statement is a very individual matter, the inspiration for medicine should be mentioned. If there are any discrepancies or idiosyncrasies in the applicant's transcript—a lot of withdrawals or some failing grades, for example—the applicant should explain in the AMCAS statement what happened. If we see something unusual in the transcripts, we will certainly ask about it during the interview, and it helps to have a written explanation beforehand.

One very common mistake is to write a statement that is too *generic*—that speaks about what the ideal physician should do or be rather than what the applicant wants to do or feels he or she should be as a physician. One has to bring it down to a personal level. Also, I do not like very flip or funny statements myself, but others may enjoy the humor. Some people have even written poetry, which I think is very ill-advised. Many applicants send us additional materials, such as audio and video tapes; one sent a scrapbook of pictures. We simply do not have the time to look at these (although we once played an audiotape as background music at a committee meeting). We just store these materials separately and forget about them, so they really are a waste of time and money.

We feel our supplementary application is very important, and we ask for four short additional paragraphs which define the person's achievements or his or her own sense of

importance. We also include a question about ethical background and its influence.

About Personal Interviews . . .

We conduct individual (not panel) interviews. We give each
candidate a minimum of two interviews (usually two or three) with
either one or two faculty members and one student. Interviews are
slated for 45 minutes to an hour each; I don't see how anyone can
conduct a meaningful interview in less time. We also conduct an
orientation which most applicants enjoy and find very helpful, and
we include lunch. So it's an all-day affair.

As for what to expect during an interview—it depends
completely on the particular interviewer. Some interviewers can be
very difficult with their interviewees; some are not. Every
interviewer develops his or her own style. A clinical physician will
probably have a different style than someone who doesn't take
care of patients. Although we don't "program" our interviews, we
do impress upon our interviewers that there are some things that
they may not ask about, such as race, religion, and plans for
marriage. We also consider ourselves "need blind" in terms of the
interview and the admissions process. So our interviewers don't
ask about the applicant's finances, either.

Conservative dress and overall appearance are suggested.
Interviewees are also advised to behave conventionally during an
interview. One candidate hauled out his candy bar and ate it in
front of the student interviewer—unbelievable, especially considering we also gave him lunch! As for freely expressing your opinions
and views, you never know if the interviewer is going to be put off
by what you say. However, if your interviewer seems to be
open-minded, you might be very well received by displaying some
"oomph" and speaking your mind. While it's hard to generalize,
in most cases having a particular line of belief and opinion makes
a far better impression than being wishy-washy, provided it is
reasonable and not radical. Most interviewers hate when someone
jumps back and forth depending on what he or she thinks the
interviewer wants.

We do schedule an orientation session for our *current* students
who will be conducting interviews. During this session our Dean of

Students, who has interviewed six or seven thousand applicants over the years, shares her advice and her experience with the students before they conduct interviews. One unusual thing about our admissions process is that we allow *first*-year students to conduct interviews after their first quarter, and we like their enthusiasm. Many schools allow only seniors to interview.

We poll our candidates immediately after their interviews. Occasionally somebody will tell us that they were not happy with an interview because inappropriate questions were asked, the line of questioning went off on a tangent, or the interviewer suddenly had to leave early. In these situations, we try to set up the applicant with another interviewer.

About the Admissions Process Generally . . .

These are the busiest years we've ever had in terms of the number of applications, and aspiring medical students should be realistic about applying. Many people who apply to medical school do so with very woeful grades and MCAT scores. They think we should let them into medical school merely because they are good people, but this is simply not the way the real world works. There are plenty of other professions that are equally satisfying. Such students should listen to their undergraduate advisors who, if they are honest, will be able to tell them that they are just not competitive and shouldn't waste their time.

The applicant's attitude in dealing with our admissions staff may actually make a difference in our admissions decision, either way. Those who are exceptionally gracious as well as those who are exceptionally arrogant are well remembered. The staff members in our office are very helpful, and when they confront an individual who is rude to them or overly demanding, we make a note of it. Our thinking is that this may represent his or her "true self." Also, when parents come to the interview or do the bulk of the calling for the student, whether or not the student knows about it, this goes against the applicant. We consider in these cases that somehow the child has not matured enough either to be let go by the parent or to take charge of his or her own decisions.

Pat Fero
Admissions Officer
School of Medicine
University of Washington

About Personal Statements . . .

At this school, when the committee members read the AMCAS personal statements they look for *motivation*—why the individual really wants to go into medicine; what really gave him or her the "call," so to speak. Applicants should give details about why they feel that they are meant for medicine and what in life or in their reading has influenced them in this direction. Perhaps someone close to the applicant was very ill once or died, and the experience with that person or with his or her doctors became very significant. After having read many statements, I believe these are the sorts of experiences that make people aware of what they themselves could do in medicine. These experiences can be very powerful material for the statement. On the other hand, a person could perhaps write about what a good doctor should be and how this fits into the overall scheme of what medicine is currently about and what health care will become in the future with all the present changes.

Many applicants make a mistake by discussing their intellectual capabilities as a major factor in being a good candidate for medicine. The applicant is reviewed at other levels in terms of his or her capability, so this should not be the focus of the personal statement. Another common misjudgment is not taking the personal statement seriously enough. Some applicants simply write a resume instead of a statement. Others try to be too cute. Candidates also get into trouble if they appear naive or overly sentimental about the medical profession and their possible role in it, projecting a "Marcus Welby" sort of feeling about being a doctor—not very realistic. The committee wants to see a general awareness of medical issues and of the medical field. An applicant might demonstrate such an awareness by talking about the problems and issues of medical care in our country—or elsewhere in the world, particularly if he or she has had the good fortune to see another health-care delivery system firsthand and is able to make a comparison.

Our supplementary application does not include open-ended essay questions. However, we do give applicants the option of submitting another personal statement with their supplementary application. Applicants should take advantage of this opportunity to show their ability to express themselves in writing but should be careful not to overdo it in terms of how much material they submit.

About In-Person Interviews . . .

We interview about 700 people for 166 available seats in our first-year class. Interviews usually last about forty minutes and are conducted by a panel of either two or three members (usually three) of the admissions committee. Interviews are "partially blinded." By this I mean that only one of the interviewers—the "executive" committee member—sees the entire current file. In the file copies provided to the other interviewers, the candidate's grades and MCAT scores are blanked out. All they know, then, about the candidate's qualifications is that he or she is either "above screen"—i.e., has a sufficiently high GPA and average score on the numerical portion of the MCAT—or has been screened and is competitive enough to be interviewed. The executive committee member is made aware of grades and MCAT scores so that he or she can ask the candidate to explain such things as dips in the GPA. The committee is looking for candidates who come across as warm and caring human beings with an awareness of medical issues and an ability to think on their feet—and not just people with strong undergraduate grades and MCAT scores.

NOTES

NOTES

Your Everything
Education Destination...

...natter where you're headed,
...he Net's largest, most
...rtant education portal.

...her you're preparing for college, gra
...l, professional school, or the workin
...l, Petersons.com is your first choice fc
...ate information and real-world advice.

...rch for the right school
...d a scholarship
...e practice admissions tests
...e interactive courses designed just for yo
...ite a better admissions essay with help
...om Harvard-educated editors

...s your future.
...t **www.petersons.com** today

...et **20% off any book** at
...eterson's Online Bookstore

www.petersons.com   Test Preparation   Financial A